omiyage

*Handmade Gifts from Fabric
in the Japanese Tradition*

Kumiko Sudo

CB
CONTEMPORARY BOOKS

Library of Congress Cataloging-in-Publication Data

Sudo, Kumiko.
    Omiyage : handmade gifts from fabric in the Japanese tradition /
Kumiko Sudo.
        p.   cm.
    ISBN 0-8092-2909-9
    1. Textile crafts—Japan.   2. Gifts—Japan.   I. Title.
TT699.S84   2000
746′.0952—dc21   00-31412
                                                      CIP

Fabrics supplied by:
Hoffman California Fabrics
Clover Needle Craft, Inc.

Editorial direction by Anne Knudsen
Project editing by Susan Moore-Kruse
Cover and interior design by Kim Bartko
Page layout by Pamela Juárez
Cover and interior photography by Sharon Hoogstraten
Calligraphy by Kumiko Sudo
Technical drawings by Kandy Petersen
Manufacturing direction by Pat Martin

Published by Contemporary Books
A division of NTC/Contemporary Publishing Group, Inc.
4255 West Touhy Avenue, Lincolnwood (Chicago), Illinois 60712-1975 U.S.A.
Printed and bound in Singapore by Star Standard Industries
International Standard Book Number: 0-8092-2909-9

01 02 03 04 05 06 SS 20 19 18 17 16 15 14 13 12 11 10 9 8 7 6 5 4 3 2

A Gift from the Heart

お土産

Enter the world of things tiny but delightful. Since early times, the Japanese have believed that God lives in all things, no matter how small. It is in the most intricate of details that the artistry of Japanese craftsmanship is most evident. We strive to make our work perfect down to the smallest detail, for it is through our arts that we celebrate life, honor nature, and offer thanks to God. A gift made from fabric is the most intimate I can give. It is made with the hands, but the good wishes it carries come only from the heart.

Kumiko Sudo

Contents

A gift made by hand and sent from the heart is the most cherished of all. In Japan, the joy of a gift is in making as well as giving it.

Delightful candy pouches, delicate evening bags, and the playful *temari* ball make exquisite gifts. All have a quiet elegance that is unmistakably Japanese.

These lovely blossoms unfold to hide tiny pockets or pouches. Each makes a perfect gift, or can be the last touch to a beautifully wrapped present.

Pretty and playful, each doll is a good luck charm, bringing goodwill and happiness to whoever receives her as a gift.

A new twist on the traditional Japanese art of "tea crafts," these lovely but oh, so useful sewing boxes and pincushions will delight anyone who loves to sew.

Soft and intimate, gifts like these promise serenity, spiritual awareness, and divine inspiration. Their sweet fragrances quiet the senses and stir the imagination.

Charming and playful, let these little woodland creatures come to life in your hands as you mold them from fabric.

Omiyage—*The Giving of Gifts*

For thousands of years, omiyage, *or the giving of gifts, has been an important part of life in Japan. Gift giving began as a means of gaining the goodwill of those in power, with those who gave gifts always subordinate to those who received them. The gift was not only a sign of respect, but a plea for protection. The rituals that surrounded gift giving were extraordinarily*

complex, with a meticulously prescribed set of protocols. Particular types of gifts were considered appropriate for particular occasions. There were detailed rules on how each should be wrapped and even presented. A mistake in selection or presentation could have dire consequences, for the lives of ordinary people were singularly dependent upon the goodwill and patronage of their lords.

Today, the formalities surrounding the giving of a gift are far less strict, yet the acts of choosing, wrapping, and presenting a gift still require careful considera-tion. For to the Japanese, a gift is an outward sign of inner feelings. It is a way in which we repay favors and acknowledge obligations, no matter how trivial. A gift is also a mark of friendship, a sign of respect, a token of deep appreciation.

It is with these thoughts in mind that I offer the gifts described in *Omiyage*. When I make a gift from fabric, I use my heart as much as my hands. I sift through the fabrics in

my collection until I find pieces with the colors and textures that I feel will please the person for whom I am making the gift. I keep those fabrics close at hand, playing with them and studying their colors and patterns, until an idea forms for the gift I wish to make. As I draw and cut and sew, I enjoy the feelings of warmth and friendship that the giving of this special token will give me. It is my wish that as you make the projects in *Omiyage*, you, too, will share the joy that comes from giving a gift from the heart.

The Art of "Small Crafts"

For centuries, Japan has been known the world over for its silks. Introduced into Japan from China in the second century B.C., Japanese silks are remarkable for their colors, textures, and elaborate designs. As early as the fourteenth century, *shogun* generals would wear battle coats made from rich imported silks, a sign of superior rank. The popularity of the tea ceremony—a ritual during which guests learn to express their appreciation of beauty—gave rise to a new art of "tea crafts." Scraps of silk, often decorated with flowers or motifs from nature, were delicately sewn into pouches used to hold tea utensils. The fabrics were cleverly crafted into shapes such as butterflies, dragonflies, cicadas, wisteria, iris, or cherry blossoms, which were often favorite symbols adopted by the *shogun* generals. The bags were tied with silk strings, made into elaborate knots that were intended to protect precious tea items from the curiosity of strangers.

Most often seen in traditional kimonos and *obi* sashes, silks have long been popular in the making of "small crafts," as they came to be known. Silks were so highly prized during the Edo period (1603 to 1867) that not even the smallest of scraps would be allowed to go to waste. Noble women would save them to make decorative purses, hair ornaments, or wrapping cloths. Women who could not afford to dress in silk kimonos would buy leftover pieces from tailors to make treasures of their own. Scraps as tiny as acorns were cleverly crafted into little good luck charms that women would tie onto the plain kimonos their children wore. Over time, silks would also be used to make all kinds of small gifts, such as coin and bill purses, tobacco pouches, or cosmetics cases.

During the Meiji period (1868 to 1912), Japan first opened its doors to the outside world. Among the many new influences from foreign cultures came a surge of interest in

In Japan, we package each gift with the utmost care, no matter how simple the gift may be. The nobles of the Heian court (794 to 1194) liked to give the gift of poetry. The delicate paper strip on which the poem was beautifully inscripted would be tucked inside a piece of Japanese rice paper, neatly folded into an *origami* shape. A twig from a blossoming plum tree would grace the gift. Upon presentation, the lucky recipient would first admire the delicacy of the wrapping, then find the poem inside.

handicrafts. This coincided with slowly changing perspectives on the social and domestic roles of women. It was through their needlework that women sought to showcase their skills. Small handicrafts became increasingly complex, as women transformed scraps of fabric into intricate, elaborately designed dolls, flowers, birds, animals, and a host of other shapes and motifs.

A wonderful tradition surrounds the birth of a new baby. In some regions of Japan, tiny scraps of fabric are collected from a hundred houses and given to the family. Each scrap represents a virtue the child will receive, and is given with prayers for the infant's health and happiness. Sometimes, tiny triangles of silk are patched together into the shape of a butterfly— a sign of rebirth, symbolizing the flight of the soul toward heaven.

The first handicrafts a young girl made would become part of her "sewing box"—a collection of small crafts that would show off to prospective husbands the girl's skill as a needlewoman. Sometimes she would give items from her box as intimate gifts to celebrate the marriage of a friend or the birth of a child. Her collection might include pouches to keep picks for musical instruments such as the *koto*, bags for personal medicines and perfumes, or secret pockets to hide a note or a poem among the folds of her kimono.

Some of my happiest childhood memories are of the years I lived with my aunt in Kamakura, a picturesque town nestled among the forested mountains at the neck of the Miura Peninsula. My aunt's house had been a *Shinto* shrine, dating back more than 800 years. It leaned against the mountainside and, for centuries, had watched over the village, safeguarding its harvests.

When friends and neighbors visited my aunt, she would send home with them a favorite gift, *sekihan*, a sticky, sweet rice cake filled with red beans. She would present this delicacy in a beautiful laquered box. When returning the box, visitors would put inside a little *origami* shape or an *otedama*—a small beanbag in the likeness of an animal or a flower, made from pretty fabrics.

My aunt loved *Noh* theater, which she taught on the sweeping verandas of the shrine. A highly skilled needlewoman, she also sewed the rich and elaborate costumes that make a *Noh* performance so distinctive. She kept leftover scraps, gilded silks in silvers and golds, in a heavy wooden chest. I liked to sit on the ancient wooden floors, those precious fabrics scattered around me, breathing in the musty but unforgettable aroma of incense and age.

One of my fondest memories is a visit I made to my aunt when I was eighteen years old. As I walked along the shady path that led to the shrine, the sweet music of the *yokobue*, a bamboo flute, rose in the air and floated toward me. There was my aunt on the veranda, gracefully dressed in an elegant kimono. A deep purple tassel tied to the flute danced to the music. At her side lay a lovely silk case for her instrument that she had crafted from the shimmering gold silks left over from a *Noh* costume she had made.

A Year of Celebration

In Japan, we often exchange gifts on special holidays and feast days. Many of our festivals date back more than 2,000 years. Some celebrate the seasons, while others are tied to the religious traditions, superstitions, and myths that make our culture so unique.

January

New Year's, *Ganjitsu*, is the most auspicious of all Japanese holidays. At the stroke of midnight on New Year's Eve, temple bells ring out to banish ill omens from the preceding year and let everyone start anew. We offer prayers for a prosperous year and watch the sun rise, greeting the new year. One of my favorite customs is the playing of *hyakunin issue*, a card game that dates back to the days of the imperial court of Kyoto (794 to 1194). Each of a hundred cards carries a poem and we recite them aloud to each other. For children, little compares with the excitement of receiving a gift of money, elaborately wrapped in decorative papers and tied with intricate knots. Prettily dressed in kimonos, they gather to fly kites or to play traditional outdoor games.

February

In Japan, we believe that every object, no matter how commonplace, has a soul, and in February we celebrate the presence of God in everything we see and touch. There is a custom among artisans of purifying the tools of their craft. They pour wine over their scissors, chisels, or knives as a means of cleansing the soul within. *Harikuyou* is a ritual of taking worn tools—tailors might take their bent or broken needles, for example—to the temple. Prayers are offered and thanks given for the contributions the tools have made.

March

In early March, when the plum trees begin to bloom, the Doll Festival, *Hina Matsuri*, begins. On a splendid red and gold dais, we display special dolls, elaborately dressed in the costumes of the Heian court (794 to 1194). The empress, usually a gift to a first granddaughter, sits on her throne next to the emperor and is surrounded by her court ladies. Intricate miniature carriages, sake sets, chests, and sewing boxes add exquisite detail to the display. Lanterns are lit and girls dressed in their prettiest kimonos gather to admire the dolls. They share a party meal and sip a sweet rice wine served only on that day. The doll ceremony is thought to protect our daughters from evil and bring them future happiness, especially in marriage.

April

From the most splendid of city parks to the poorest of fishing villages, the Japanese welcome the spring by viewing the pink waves of cherry trees in bloom. *Sakura Matsuri* has been celebrated since ancient times and has inspired many of our greatest poets and artists. We dress in lovely flowered kimonos and share a picnic in the cherry groves. Delicate pink and white blossoms fall around us, a gentle reminder that beauty and joy are fleeting. The buds burst into bloom and, within a few short sweet days, they are gone.

May

Tango No Sekku, on May 5, was once a day to honor boys but is now known as Children's Day. High above the rooftops, houses with sons hoist very unusual streamers that take the shape of giant carp—a most auspicious fish that signifies strength and courage. Swimming in the wind, high in the blue sky, the brightly colored carp urge boys to swim upstream, persevering toward their goals against all odds. We also celebrate the day by displaying miniature flags, helmets, or armor in the home. Iris leaves, believed to ward off evil and bring good health, are placed beneath the eaves or are used to scent the bath.

June

In June, we pray for rain and for a rich rice harvest. Rice is still the staple food of Japan and is of vital importance to our well-being. The hydrangea are in bloom, creating a sea of blue and purple blossoms on the steps of the shrines, as people make offerings in thanks for rain. In June, we celebrate the changing of the seasons, airing out winter clothes and packing them away for summer. When I was a child, my mother would untie the stitching in our kimonos so that she could wash and starch each piece of fabric. She would leave them to dry on long wooden boards in the eaves of the house, where we would happily play hide and seek, peeking out from the fresh, flowing fabrics.

July

Summer is a time of joy and festivity, and we celebrate many special days with dance, music, and games. *Tanabata*, the Autumn Star Festival, is inspired by the legend of two lovers—the stars Altair, personified as a cowherd, and Vega, a weaving girl. Separated by the Milky Way for the rest of the year, they cross the night skies each summer for a lover's tryst. Children write their wishes on strips of colorful paper and hang them on bamboo branches placed at the gates of the home. Women, too, ask Vega to help them improve their sewing skills!

August

The feast of *O'bon* is dedicated to the souls of our ancestors. We return to our hometowns to tend to the graves of loved ones. At neighborhood temples and shrines, bonfires are built to welcome back departed souls and guide them to their families. All night long, by the light of hundreds of lanterns, dancers dressed in summer kimonos move to the beat of a drum. After three days, the spirits are sent on their journey back to heaven.

September

Since the beginning of the Nara period (710 to 794), we have honored the full moon. Court nobles would exchange poetry, with the moon as their muse. Through the ages, we have prayed to the moon for a good harvest. I remember moon-viewing as a child. My mother would make special rice cakes and send me to collect pampas grass to decorate our dishes. We would sit on the veranda, trying to make out the shape of a rabbit—just as in the West, children look for the man in the moon. In Japan, the rabbit is thought to be a fairy creature, sent by the moon.

October

Kiku, the chrysanthemum, was introduced from China in 325 A.D. In the year 797, the emperor Kan-mu held a banquet at which the entire court was decorated with the sweetly scented flower, believed to keep away evil influences and entice benevolent spirits. Chrysanthemum wine was served, and dances, music, and poetry were offered in praise of this lovely flower. Since then, the imperial families have decorated their clothing and carriages with the chrysanthemum emblem. Sixteen petals radiating from the center like the rays of the sun make this an ideal imperial motif, for historically the emperor was regarded as divine, a living god. In October, festivals celebrate the chrysanthemum, with prizes for the most perfect of blooms.

November

Shichi-go-san (translated as "seven-five-three," which are lucky numbers in Japan) is the occasion when parents take children who are three, five, or seven years old to the shrine to give thanks for their health and to pray for their futures. The children are dressed in colorful kimonos, like bright flowers among the autumn trees.

December

December is the busiest month of the year, as we try to tie up loose ends so that we can make a clean start in the new year. Mid-month, *Kotohajime*, is the time that we clean out the temple, the shrine, and the home. The great statue of Buddha in the ancient city of Nara is carefully dusted and shined. We begin writing New Year's greeting cards and preparing special foods for the holiday. At midnight on New Year's Eve, the temple bells ring out, casting away the 108 evil passions that, according to Buddhist belief, take over the mind during the year. We listen to the bells with honest hearts and are ready to begin anew.

Notes on Technique

In *Omiyage* you will find forty-five gift ideas that you
can make from fabrics. Some are very simple and can be
completed in an hour or less. *Daffodil, Fortune Catcher,* or
Tsuru, for example, are all easy to make. Others may take a
little more time and a little more practice, yet these are the
ones that will surprise and delight you the most.

Choosing Fabrics

Many of the designs photographed are made from small
scraps of fabrics in my collection. Some are made from
exquisite Japanese silks; others are made from contemporary
American cottons. Some are made from special *shibori*
fabrics or *chiromen* crepes, used to make Japanese scarves.

 I am a quiltmaker, and—like every quilter I know—
I have scraps upon scraps of fabrics in my workroom that I
like so much I cannot bear to throw them away, no matter
how tiny they are. Sometimes, I buy a length of fabric
simply because I cannot resist the colors, the textures, or a
detail in the design. I love the look and feel of Japanese kimonos and have cut up
many of them so that I can incorporate their rich colors and swirling patterns into
my designs. I am fortunate that people all over the world who have seen my work
send me unusual pieces of fabric that they think I will like.

 To make the projects in *Omiyage*, you do not need to start with a large fabric
collection, nor do you need to spend a lot of money. All of the projects can be
made out of very small pieces and you can easily mix and match fabrics within a
single design. For each project, I have suggested how much fabric you will need, but
these quantities are always overly generous. A ⅛ yd (15cm) length, for example, will
often allow enough fabric for two, three, or more of the projects you are making.
Using the photographs as a guide to contrast (the use of light, medium, and dark
tones), I suggest you choose colors and patterns that you enjoy. It is your
combinations that will make your gifts unique.

Cutting

Full-size patterns are provided for all pieces other than simple squares and
rectangles. To all patterns, unless otherwise indicated on the pattern piece or in the

Basic Tool Kit

A list of materials is supplied with every
project. In addition, for most projects you will
need the items listed here. Collect everything
you need before you start and keep them in a
box or basket within easy reach. A little
preparation will save you time and frustration
when you sit down to make a new project.

Hand-sewing needles	Craft knife and
Pins and pincushion	replacement blades
Thimble	Self-healing cutting mat
High-quality hand-	Eraser
sewing threads	Sharp pencils
in variety of colors	Disappearing pen
Cotton/polyester	Charcoal marker
batting	All-purpose glue or
Sharp fabric scissors	glue stick
Paper scissors	Ruler
Thread snips	Tape measure
Compass	Tracing paper

sewing directions, you will need to add a ¼″ (0.75cm) seam allowance. In some instances, where the pattern pieces are very small, this is reduced to a ⅛″ (0.4cm) seam allowance. For squares and rectangles, the measurements in the sewing directions already include seam allowances. Most of the pattern pieces are curved, which means they are easier to cut with very sharp scissors than with rotary cutting equipment. Since the projects are small and multiples of the same pattern piece are rarely needed, hand-cutting is quick and easy. Remember to transfer any markings from the pattern onto the cut pieces of fabric.

Several of the projects, including the gift boxes, require you to cut the patterns from cardboard as well as fabric. Do not add seam allowances when cutting cardboard pieces. Use a stiff, high-quality cardboard that does not bend or tear easily. Choose white or a light color to avoid the cardboard showing through thin fabrics.

Sewing

I sew everything—straight seams and curved seams, piecing and appliqué—by hand. I feel that the hand is directed not only by the eye but by the heart. When I make gifts, I like the sense of intimacy that hand-sewing gives me. Since all the projects in *Omiyage* are small, you may want to sew by hand, too. If you prefer to sew by machine, you will find that straight seams in simple piecing projects like *Panache!* or *Candy Twist* turn out beautifully. In certain projects, however, where you may need to manipulate the fabric as you sew, you may find that hand-sewing is not only faster, but more accurate. *Playtime!*, *Edo Temari*, and *Oyster* all require special care.

Many of the designs involve sewing curved seams. For perfect curved seams, I use a form of appliqué. My technique involves placing a fabric piece, with the seam allowance folded under, on top of a background piece; the piece is then blind-stitched by hand. In the instructions, this is what is meant by the term *appliqué*. The term *sew* indicates a more traditional method of sewing the pieces together, right sides facing, using a running stitch on the wrong side of the seam lines. Straight seams are sewn in this way, and you may use hand or machine stitching.

Fabric Origami

Many of the projects in *Omiyage* are inspired by the Japanese art of *origami*, or paper folding. As a child, I loved the colors and patterns in decorative *origami* papers and would mold them into shapes of my own. Now, instead of paper, I fold fabrics. Even if you know nothing of *origami*, you will find that my fabric-folding techniques are easy to learn. These tips may help.

- Study each folding diagram carefully before you begin. Determine which is the right and wrong side of the fabric. Practice each new shape on a sample so that you solve any difficulties before you begin on your final piece.
- Always fold accurately and neatly.
- Crease each fold firmly with the back of your thumbnail. Good creases make the folding easier, and they serve as guides to future steps.
- One difference between folding paper and folding fabric is that paper is available with different colors on the two sides. To achieve the same effect with fabric, first sew two colors together, then turn them right side out and press. Often, finger pressing will be adequate.

You will find that the same procedures are used over and over again. You will soon become so proficient with them that you can do them without thinking.

Making Hems for Purses and Pouches

Several of the purses and pouches in *Omiyage* have hem pieces that wrap from the inside, lined pocket to the outside. Here is the method I use to make hems. The patterns will refer you back to this section when needed.

1. Cut two hem pieces to sizes directed in pattern.
2. Fold in ends of each by ½″ (1.5cm). Fold in half lengthwise, right side out. Turn in seam allowances and press in place.
3. Right sides together, stitch first hem piece to bag. Add second hem piece, taking care not to overlap edges.
4. Fold hem piece over to inside. Blindstitch in place.
5. Insert two ribbons or drawstrings, cut to lengths specified in pattern. Thread both through both sides of bag hem. Knot ends.

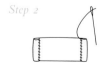
Step 2

Step 3

Step 4

Making Fabric Beads

The ribbons that you use to close many of the purses and pouches in *Omiyage* are decorated with soft beads made out of pretty fabrics. I use several methods to make them, each with a slightly different look. I will refer you back to this section when needed. For bulkier beads, stuff with a little batting before pulling stitches tight.

Method 1

1. Cut two fabric squares to sizes directed in pattern. Place a thin layer of batting onto wrong side of each square.
2. Fold under each edge, finger press, and baste in place. Make a single gathering stitch at the center point of each edge. If desired, stuff with more batting while pulling gathering stitches gently to hold.
3. Stuff knotted ends of ribbons or drawstrings inside fabric bead. Pull gathering stitches tight. Double-stitch to hold.

Step 1   *Step 2*   *Step 3*

Method 2

1. Cut two fabric squares to sizes directed in pattern.
2. Fold in half and stitch as shown, trapping end of ribbon above knot inside. Turn right side out, pulling over knot.
3. Fold under bottom edge by ⅝″ (1.8cm). Gather-stitch, pulling thread tight. Backstitch to hold.

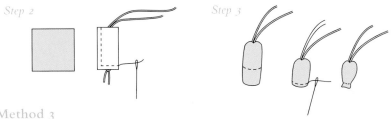

Step 2   *Step 3*

Method 3

1. Cut two strips of fabric to sizes directed in pattern.
2. Join seam along longest edge to create tube. Wrong side out. Slip over knotted end of ribbon.

3. Gather-stitch edge closest to knot and pull tightly. Backstitch to hold.
4. Turn right side out, pulling over knot. Fold raw edge under by ¼″ (0.75cm). Stitch around loop and pull tight to gather, enclosing knot. Backstitch to hold. For bulkier bead, stuff with a little batting before pulling stitches tight.

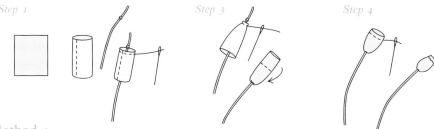

Step 1 *Step 3* *Step 4*

Method 4

1. Cut two squares of fabric to sizes directed in pattern.
2. Fold in all raw edges by ⅛″ (0.4cm) and stitch. Fold in half along diagonal to create triangle.
3. Place knot of ribbon or drawstring inside triangle. Fold in half again to make smaller triangle.
4. Blindstitch all edges, enclosing knot.
5. Bring tips of triangle together and stitch.

Step 2 *Step 4* *Step 5*

Method 5

1. Cut two circles of fabric as directed in pattern.
2. Fold in half and stitch from A to B. Open out. Fold again and stitch from C to D. Open out.
3. Stitch around entire outer edge of circle and pull to gather. Stuff with batting.
4. Put knotted ends of ribbon or drawstring inside bud. Pull gathering stitches tight. Double-stitch to hold.

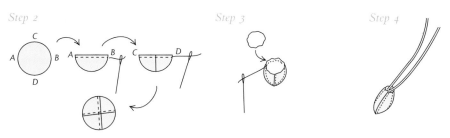

Step 2 *Step 3* *Step 4*

Decorative Knots

A distinctively Japanese feature of several of the projects is the elaborate knots used to tie cords or ribbons. The following diagrams will help you tie knots like these with ease.

To Make a Josephine Knot

To begin, first fold the cord in half to mark the center point. I find it easiest to loop the midpoint around a pencil to hold it securely in place. The left tail of the cord is shaded; the right tail is unshaded. Follow the diagrams to make the knot, pulling tight when complete.

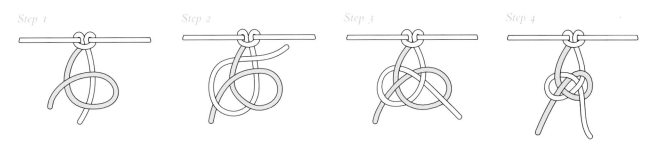

Step 1 *Step 2* *Step 3* *Step 4*

To Make a Square Knot

To begin, pin one end of each of two strands of cord to a corkboard, or tape them to a desk surface, to hold them securely in place. The strand beginning at the right is shaded; the left strand is not. Follow the diagrams to make the knot, pulling tight when complete.

To make a chain of square knots, knot several in succession, pulling tight after each one.

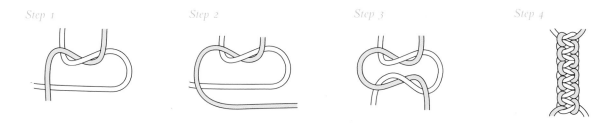

Step 1 *Step 2* *Step 3* *Step 4*

To Make a Blossom Knot

To begin, first fold the cord in half to mark the center point. Put a pin through the center point and pin to a corkboard or a large pincushion to hold it securely in place. Follow the diagrams to complete the knot. The left tail of the cord is shaded; the right tail is unshaded.

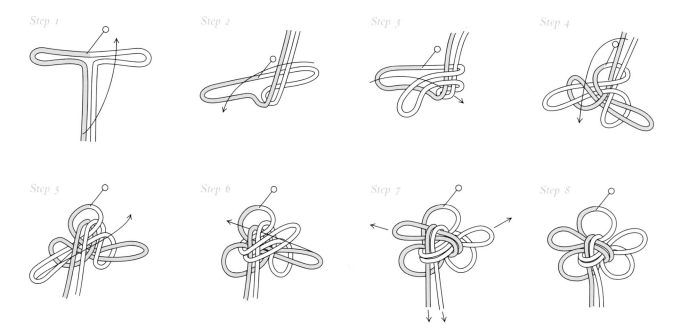

Step 1   Step 2   Step 3   Step 4

Step 5   Step 6   Step 7   Step 8

omiyage

Kyoto Chic

享都の粋

Ah, Kyoto! City of light, city of majesty. From her broad, sweeping avenues to her cobbled streets and picturesque bridges, Kyoto is the heart and soul of Japanese style. For more than 1,100 years Kyoto was the imperial capital, and it is here that the exquisite artistry that is so uniquely Japanese developed. When the court moved to Tokyo in

1194, Kyoto remained a glittering city of waterways, palaces, temples, and shrines.

Since ancient times, Kyoto has been a center for silk weaving, embroidery, and other fiber arts, and today the city still offers the utmost in sophistication in all matters of fashion. A kimono made in Kyoto is finer than any other imaginable, and the city's elite boutiques open their doors to the most stylish of clientele.

As you browse the projects in this chapter, a word to remember is *shibui*. It describes the power of tranquility to create beauty, especially out of ordinary things. The projects are simple—pretty candy pouches, delicate evening bags, a stylish brooch pin, and the playful *temari* ball. Yet in combining colorful fabrics and pleasing textures to make them, you will discover the quiet elegance that is so much a part of Japanese high fashion—understated, yet oh, so chic!

Marbles

Made up in three exotic fabrics, this little pouch is perfect for a small collection of favorite marbles, or for any special treasure.

1. Cut thirty strips, each measuring 6″ × 1¼″ (15.5cm × 3.4cm). Use patterned fabric for half and a solid color for half.

2. Right sides together, stitch one patterned strip to one solid strip. Continue adding strips, alternating patterns and solids and alternating direction of seam.

3. Join end strips together to make a loop. Fold each patterned strip in half vertically so that it is hidden beneath and between solid strips. Press gently in place. Baste around top to hold. Gather-stitch around bottom. Pull stitches tight and backstitch to hold.

4. Cut a circle of fabric measuring 2″ (5cm) in diameter. Gather-stitch ¼″ (0.75cm) from edge. Stuff with batting or fabric scraps and pull thread tight until stuffed circle measures about ½″ (1.5cm) in diameter. Backstitch to hold. Position on bottom of bag, covering gathers. Stitch in place.

5. Cut a strip for lining, measuring 5½″ × 15″ (14.5cm × 38cm). Right sides together, fold in half lengthwise and stitch seam. Baste along bottom edge and pull thread tight to gather. Backstitch to hold. Wrong sides together, position lining inside bag. Pin and stitch in place around top edge, working in any extra fullness as you go.

6. Cut two hem pieces measuring 1½″ × 7½″ (4cm × 19.4cm). Follow directions for making hems on page xvi.

7. To create fabric beads, cut out squares of fabric measuring 2″ × 2″ (5.4cm × 5.4cm). Follow directions for Method 1 on page xvii.

Materials

Solid fabric, ¼ yd (25cm)
  or less

Patterned fabric, ¼ yd (25cm)
  or less

Fabric for lining, ¼ yd (25cm)
  or less

Cotton/polyester batting

Two 24″ (60cm) ribbons or
  drawstrings

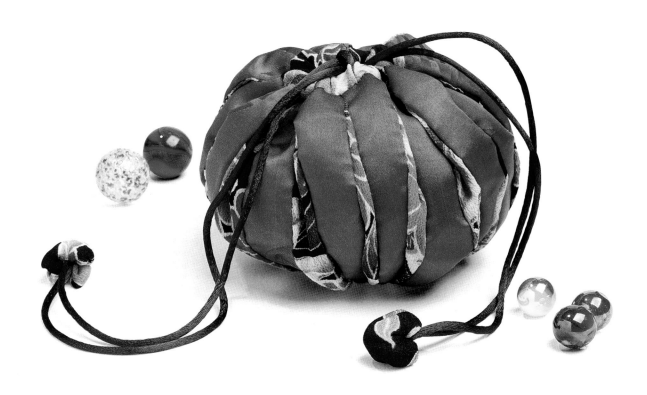

Use ¼" (0.75cm) allowance for all seams.

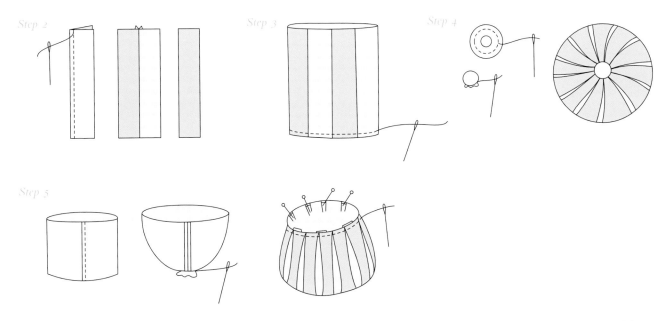

Step 2

Step 3

Step 4

Step 5

Panache!

Colorful, light, and so very chic, Panache! *lends a little oriental flair to even the most casual of fashions.*

1. Using Pattern A, cut six. Cut twelve strips measuring 2¼″ × 4″ (6cm × 10.6cm). Mark center of longer edge of each strip.

2. Right sides together, sew a diagonal edge of A to a short edge of first strip. Stitch line stops ¼″ (0.75cm) from raw edges, as shown. Right sides together, align second strip to center mark of first strip as shown. Stitch seam, again stopping ¼″ (0.75cm) from edges.

3. Add third strip to first two, aligning as shown with center mark on second strip, again stopping ¼″ (0.75cm) from edges. This completes the first unit.

4. Join second A piece to a new strip, as in Step 2. Right sides together, join this new unit to first unit, as shown. Begin stitching at bottom of strip, swiveling the fabric gently to make your way around the angle. Add next strip, aligning along bottom edge of unit and at center mark.

5. Repeat Step 4 until all A pieces and strips are connected, stitching last pieces to first unit to form a tube with six "triangles" of fabric at bottom.

6. Fold in triangles, pin together, and stitch seams to form outer pouch. Turn right side out. To keep bottom of bag firm, use Pattern B (no seam allowance) to cut a circle from cardboard, and insert into bottom of bag.

7. Cut a 5″ × 18″ (13cm × 43.2cm) strip for lining. Stitch short edges together to form tube. Using Pattern B and lining fabric, cut bottom. Right sides together, pin and then stitch bottom to tube to form inner pouch. Place lining inside bag. Pin and baste in place along top edges, working in any extra fullness as you go.

8. Cut two strips measuring 2″ × 9″ (5.4m × 23cm) for hem. Follow directions for making hems on page xvi.

9. To create fabric beads, cut two squares of fabric measuring 2″ × 2″ (5cm × 5cm). Follow directions for Method 2 on page xvii.

Materials

Patterned fabric for outer bag, hem, and beads, ½ yd (50cm) or less

Fabric for lining, ½ yd (50cm) or less

Two 26″ (66cm) ribbons or drawstrings

Sheet of cardboard

Patterns on page 109. Use ¼" (0.75cm) allowance for all seams.

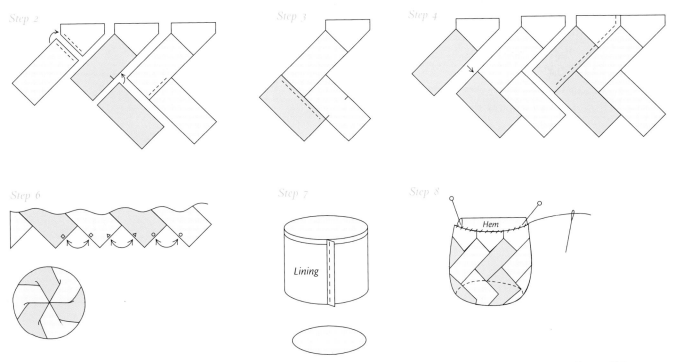

Step 2

Step 3

Step 4

Step 6

Step 7

Lining

Step 8

Hem

Sea Bream Dream

Since Japan is an island nation, fish have been a popular motif in its arts and legends and denote good fortune. This purse, with its sweeping curves and playful lines, is a gift of energy and lasting harmony.

1. Using Pattern A, cut two from fabric and two from interfacing. Transfer markings onto fabric. Baste or fuse interfacing to wrong side of each bag piece.

2. Cut strips as follows:
   Cut two measuring 1″ × 5″ (2.5cm × 13cm)
   Cut two measuring 1″ × 7½″ (2.5cm × 19.4cm)
   Cut one measuring 1″ × 6½″ (2.5cm × 16.8cm)
   Fold in all edges, press, and pin in position on bag front. Make sure there is an even space of 1″ (2.5cm) between strips. Blindstitch all edges.

3. Cut one from Pattern B and two from Pattern C, adding seam allowance of ⅛″ (0.4cm) or less. Turn under seam allowance and appliqué in position on bag front, overlapping strips as shown in photograph. To make button, cut one from Pattern D. Gather-stitch, stuffing with a little batting, and appliqué in position over tips of previous pieces. Alternatively, use a decorative button. Add decorative stitching using gold or silver metallic thread as shown.

4. Cut fish pieces using Patterns E, F, and G, adding ⅛″ (0.4cm) seam allowance. For head G, use fabric with large flower at center, as in photograph. Pin gill F on top of body E, matching curve. Appliqué sides and bottom edge, turning under seam allowance. Right sides together, stitch head G to body and gill.

Materials

Assorted patterned fabrics for bag front and back, fish, flower, and fabric beads, ½ yd (50cm) or less

Fabric for lining, ¼ yd (25cm) or less

Fusible or non-fusible interfacing, ¼ yd (25cm) or less

Two 46″ (116cm) decorative cords or drawstrings

Cotton/polyester batting

Metallic thread or embroidery floss

2″ (5cm) thin string or thick thread

Patterns on pages 110–113. Use ¼″ (0.75cm) allowance for all seams.

Step 2

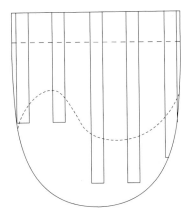

Step 3

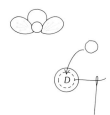

Step 4

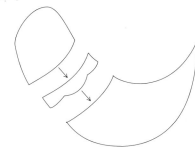

5. Cut and appliqué remaining fish pieces H to T in alphabetical order, using ⅛″ (0.4cm) seam allowance or less. (Note: There are two S pieces.)

6. Using gold or silver metallic thread or embroidery floss, add embellishments in decorative stitch, as shown. Create a button loop by attaching 2″ (5cm) string or thread to top of fish, hiding tails behind Pattern M. Adjust size of loop to fit button.

7. Using Pattern U, cut fish lining, transferring curved line and dots. Right sides together, stitch top of lining to top of fish, sewing along curve and making sure stitches do not extend beyond dots. Trap ends of button loop between fish body and lining. Turn right side out.

8. Cut eight squares measuring 1½″ × 1½″ (4cm × 4cm). Fold across diagonal three times to create small triangle. Slide fabric slightly to allow about ⅛″ (0.4cm) of bottom layer to show. Pin and then baste fins in position onto back of fish along bottom curve. Pin fish to bag front, matching curves.

9. Slip-stitch from top left triangle around entire head. Right sides together, stitch bag front to back, matching curve. Leave top open. Turn right side out. Fold top edge inward along fold line. Baste in place.

10. Using Pattern V, cut lining, transferring fold line. Right sides together, sew back and front lining together, leaving top open. Do not turn right side out. Fold and press top edge outward along fold line. Insert lining into bag. Adjust

Step 5

Step 6

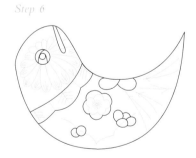

Step 8

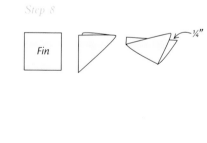

so that top edge of lining lies about ½″ (1.5cm) below top edge of bag. Pin in place and slip-stitch top edges together. Remove all basting.

11. Using Pattern W and adding ⅛″ (0.4cm) seam allowance, cut twenty tails. Stitch two tails, right sides together, leaving ½″ (1.5cm) opening. Turn right side out. Make total of ten. Fold tip forward along fold line. Stitch ⅜″ (1cm) from top through both layers along fold line to create tube.

12. Pin five tails in position along front and five along back of bag. Attach as close as possible to top edge of bag, stitching over previous stitch line. Insert one drawstring through front five loops and one through back five loops. Knot together at either end.

13. To create fabric beads, cut squares of fabric measuring 2¼″ × 2¼″ (5.6cm × 5.6cm). Follow directions for Method 1 on page xvii.

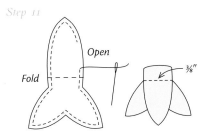

Step 11

Open

Fold

⅜″

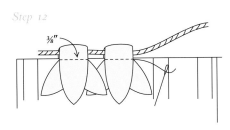

Step 12

⅜″

Candy Twist

Everyone loves a gift of candy, and there is no prettier presentation than the Candy Twist *pouch. Place one at a table setting and let each guest take a lovely bag of treats home.*

1. Cut thirty-six strips of fabric, each measuring 1¼″ × 6″ (3.4cm × 15.5cm). Use dark fabric for first twelve, light for next twelve, and checkered fabric for rest.
2. Right sides together, stitch one dark to one light along one long edge. Turn right side out and fold along seam. Press. Make twelve pairs.
3. Insert dark/light pair between two checkered pieces, then sew right side raw edges together. Continue adding checkered strips to dark/light pairs, alternating direction of seams to reduce stretching of fabric.
4. Join end strips together to make a loop. Turn right side out. Baste around top.
5. Gently pull light/dark pairs apart to reveal checkered strips. Press top halves of light/dark pairs to right and bottom halves to left to create twist effect.
6. Gather-stitch around bottom of bag. Cover a ¾″ (2cm) button with patterned fabric. Position on bottom of bag to cover gathers. Stitch in place.
7. Cut a strip of fabric for lining, measuring 5″ × 12″ (12.8cm × 30cm). Right sides together, fold in half lengthwise and stitch seam. Baste along bottom edge

Materials

⅛ yd (15cm) or less each of dark patterned fabric, light patterned fabric, and checkered fabric

Fabric for lining, ¼ yd (25cm) or less

Two 29″ (75cm) ribbons or drawstrings

¾″ (2cm) button

Fabric scraps or cotton/polyester batting

Use ¼″ (0.75cm) allowance for all seams.

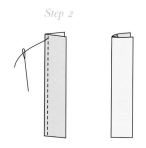

Step 2

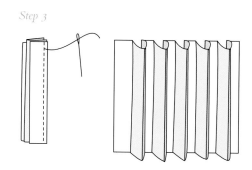

Step 3

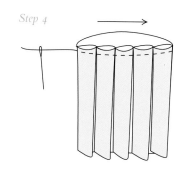

Step 4

and pull thread tight to gather. Backstitch to hold. Wrong sides together, position lining inside bag. Pin and stitch in place around top edge, working in any extra fullness as you go.

8. Cut two hem pieces measuring 1½″ × 6″ (4cm × 15cm). Follow directions for making hems on page xvi.

9. To create fabric beads, cut two squares of fabric measuring 1¼″ × 1¼″ (3.2cm × 3.2cm). Follow directions for Method 2 on page xvii.

Step 6

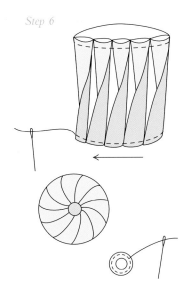

Step 7

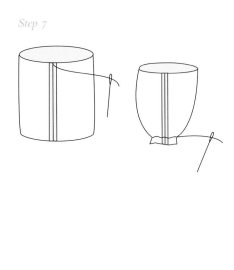

Temari

Temari balls are a favorite among Japanese children and are so pretty they suit even the most formal of occasions. There are few sights as joyful as a small child in a kimono gaily tossing a temari ball into the air.

1. Using fabric shreds or scraps, wad a tightly packed ball in your hands, building on it until it is about 4″ (10cm) in diameter. Wrap it in a layer of batting and secure by wrapping again and again with dental floss. Add another layer of batting, securing in same way. Final ball should be about 5¼″ (13cm) from center top to center bottom. It is fine if shape is a little uneven—that is one of the pleasures of creating this unique handmade ball.

2. Using Pattern A, cut fourteen pieces from five favorite fabrics. Fold in and press seam allowance along one raw edge at right side of each piece.

3. Pin first piece to ball, stretching to make it reach from top center to bottom center. Position, stretch, and pin second piece over raw edge of first piece. Stitch in place.

4. Continue adding remaining pieces over raw edge of preceding piece. To stitch final piece, tuck raw edge under folded edge of first piece. Note: Depending on final size of ball, you may need one or more extra pieces. Do not worry about neatness of top center and bottom center where pieces join; these will be covered.

Materials

Five assorted patterned fabrics for ball, each ⅛ yd (15cm) or less

Fabric for belt, ⅛ yd (15cm) or less

Three assorted patterned fabrics for petals, ⅛ yd (15cm) or less

Fabric for flower core, scrap

Fabric shreds or scraps

Cotton/polyester batting

Dental floss or lace tatting

Patterns on page 114. Use ¼″ (0.75cm) allowance for all seams.

Step 1

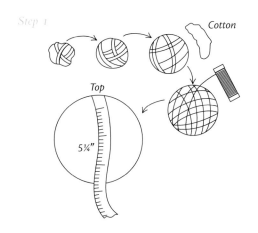

Cotton

Top

5¼″

Step 2

Step 3

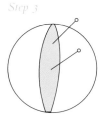

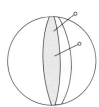

5. Using Pattern B, cut one hexagon, adding ⅛″ (0.4cm) seam allowance. Fold under and press seam allowance in place. Stitch hexagon to bottom of ball.

6. Cut fabric strip measuring 1¼″ × 12″ (3.2cm × 30cm) for belt. Fold into thirds horizontally, as shown. Pin around center line of ball. Slip-stitch around entire top and bottom edges.

7. Using Pattern C and three complementary fabrics, cut twenty-five flower petals. Do not add seam allowance. Fold each three times as shown. Stitch and gather as shown. Backstitch to hold.

8. Using Pattern D and adding ⅛″ (0.4cm) seam allowance, cut five flower core pieces. Fold under and press seam allowance. Arrange five petals with flower core pinned in position at center. Stitch in place.

9. Arrange completed flowers on ball, with four at equal intervals around belt and one at top of ball.

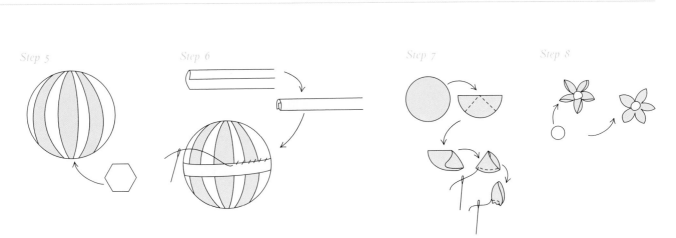

Step 5   Step 6   Step 7   Step 8

Dutch Cat

This exquisite purse sets off an elegant evening gown to perfection. Highly prized in ancient times, cats are thought to possess supernatural powers. Dutch Cat *brings a little magic to any occasion.*

1. Using Pattern A, cut two for bag and two for lining. Cut cat pieces B to I, reducing seam allowance to ⅛" (0.4cm) for smaller pieces. Pattern F has no seam allowance. Transfer face, tail, and paw markings from Pattern B, and paw markings from Patterns H and I.

2. Position cat body B on bag front and pin in place. Fold seam allowances under and appliqué onto bag. Appliqué tail C onto body, tucking a 5" (13cm) length of string inside as you sew. Appliqué collar D and ball E in place.

3. Fold ears F in half, then fold again. Gather-stitch curved raw edge. Pull stitches to gather and backstitch to hold. Sew onto body, aligning with curve of collar.

4. Cut two strips measuring 1" × 3½" (2.5cm × 9cm) for necktie. Right sides together, fold lengthwise and sew seam, leaving 1" (2.5cm) opening. Turn right side out. Blindstitch opening closed. Gather-stitch 1" (2.5cm) from bottom edge of each tube. Make a fringe by folding an 8" (20cm) strand of thread multiple times until it measures about 1" (2.5cm). Tie tight at center. Cut loops. Insert center of fringe into necktie tube. Fold in raw edges and pull gathering stitches tight, trapping fringe inside tube. Backstitch to hold. Appliqué necktie around curve of left and right chin as shown in photograph. Double-tie ends.

5. Embroider eyes, nose, and mouth onto face G. Fold seam allowance under and appliqué face in position, stuffing with a little batting as you sew.

6. Right sides together, sew around matching paw pieces H and I, leaving top open. Turn right side out. Stuff with batting. Stitch along paw markings.

7. Right sides together, sew back and front of bag together, leaving top open. Repeat for lining, but do not turn right side out. Insert lining into bag. Fold and press raw edges of bag and lining inward, making top edge of lining slightly lower than top edge of bag. Tuck paws between bag and lining. Pin in place.

8. Fold each cord or decorative string in half, marking center point with pin. Tuck ends in position between bag and lining. Pin in place. Blindstitch along folded-in seam allowances, attaching lining to bag and securing paws and cords. Sew small bell, button, or other decoration below necktie. To add decorative blossom knot shown in photograph, see page xx.

Materials

Assorted patterned fabrics for bag, cat, collar, necktie, and ball, ½ yd (50cm) or less

Fabric for lining, ¼ yd (25cm) or less

5" (13cm) string

Two 20" (50cm) decorative cords

Cotton/polyester batting

Embroidery floss

Small bell, button, or other decoration

Patterns on pages 114–116. Use ¼" (0.75cm) allowance for all seams.

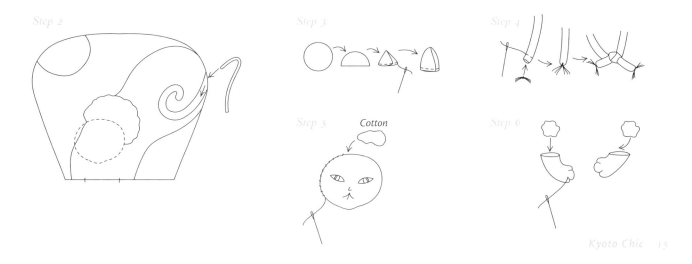

Step 2

Step 3

Step 4

Step 5   Cotton

Step 6

Oyster

Pinned to your lapel, this pincushion—cleverly crafted from a shell—allows you to keep stitching, even when dressed to the nines! Remove the pins, and voilà! A little brooch of uncommon elegance.

1. Position shell on fabric and cut around it, adding generous ½″ (1.5cm) seam allowance. Gather-stitch around all edges. Smear craft glue around top outside and inside edges of shell and place inside gathered fabric. Pull gathering stitches tight, finger pressing lightly to stick to glue. Backstitch to hold. Shell should be covered evenly, with no puckers.

2. Fold cord in half and pin folded tip. Make decorative Josephine knot, as described on page xix. Make two or three stitches about 1½″ (4cm) below Josephine knot to secure two tails of cord together. Position cord on underside of covered shell as shown and glue in place. Knot end of each tail.

3. Using Pattern A, cut one flower piece. Gather-stitch around edges. Stuff with batting until firm and pull stitches tight. Double-stitch to hold.

4. Secure decorative thread with double-stitch on back of flower piece. Draw thread evenly over and across front and back four times so that surface is divided into eight pie-shaped sections. Double-stitch again on back to hold. Make a fringe by folding a 12″ (30cm) strand of thread multiple times until it measures about 1″ (2.5cm). Tie tight at center. Cut loops. Stitch center of fringe to center of flower pieces where threads criss-cross.

Materials

Small sea shell—shell photographed measures about 1½″ × 2″ (4cm × 5cm)

Decorative fabric for shell cover and flower, ⅛ yd (15cm) or less

20″ (50cm) decorative cord

Cotton/polyester batting

Decorative thread, such as gold metallic thread or embroidery floss

1″ × 11″ (2.5cm × 28cm) bias strip or silk ribbon

Craft glue

Patterns on page 116. Use ¼″ (0.75cm) allowance for all seams.

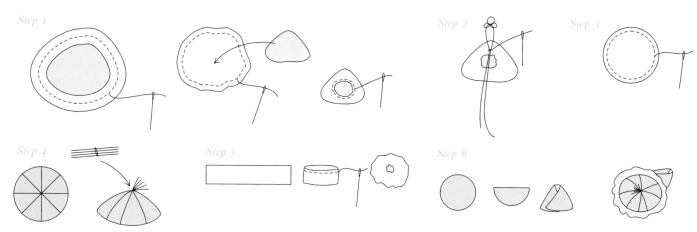

Step 1

Step 2

Step 3

Step 4

Step 5

Step 6

5. Prepare a 1″ × 11″ (2.5cm × 28cm) bias strip or use length of silk ribbon. Stitch ends to make loop. Gather-stitch one edge and pull stitches gently to create frill. Sew frilled bias to bottom of flower.

6. Using Pattern B, cut leaf. Do not add seam allowance. Fold into three and gather-stitch curved edge. Pull tight and double-stitch to hold. Sew leaf to underside of frill.

7. Glue flower and leaf securely inside shell, pressing in place for at least two minutes.

Variation

For a flat, non-cushioned surface, first prepare shell and cord as in Steps 1 to 3. Next, cut a shape the same size as your shell from light cardboard. Wrap with fabric and glue in place. Embellish with 30″ (76cm) strand of decorative thread, drawing thread across card as shown, imitating grooves in sea shell. Place in shell, gluing ends of thread to inside of shell to hide. Glue in place. Make a small Josephine knot in each of two 8″ (20cm) lengths of decorative cord (see page xix). Knot tails of each cord. Stitch in place on top edge of shell.

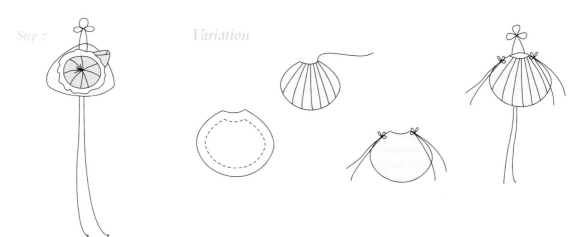

Step 7   Variation

Empress

Worn as a purse or draped over a dresser, Empress *brings an elegance that is unmistakably Japanese.*

1. Using Pattern A, cut one from cardboard; cut one from white cotton for face, adding ⅛″ (0.4cm) seam allowance. Cut small rectangle of cardboard measuring ½″ × 1″ (1.5cm × 2.5cm); cut rectangle measuring ¾″ × 1¼″ (2cm × 3.2cm) from white cotton for neck. Place thin layer of batting over each cardboard piece. Gather-stitch around fabric face. For each piece, insert cardboard, batting side up, inside fabric and pull stitches tight. Backstitch to hold. Fold over and glue seam allowance to reverse side of cardboard, trapping layer of batting inside.

2. Using fine-tip marker, lightly draw or embroider features onto face.

3. Cut three collar pieces from three different fabrics (match fabric to bag and sleeves), measuring as follows: top collar: ¾″ × 3″ (2cm × 7.6cm); middle collar: ¾″ × 3½″ (2cm × 9cm); bottom collar: 1½″ × 3½″ (4cm × 9cm). Fold in half lengthwise. Glue top collar around neck line; glue middle collar beneath, overlapping edges so that ⅛″ (0.4cm) of top collar shows; glue bottom collar, overlapping edges so that ⅛″ (0.4cm) of middle collar shows.

4. Using Patterns B to F, cut two of each hair piece from black fabric, except cut only one from Pattern D. Add ⅛″ (0.4cm) seam allowances; increase seam allowance to ¼″ (0.75cm) for bottom edge of B only. Match pairs and stitch, right sides together, leaving about ½″ (1.5cm) opening. Turn right side out. Blindstitch opening closed. Place C on top of B, matching curve. Blindstitch all edges. Position neck and collar on top and blindstitch. Add face in same way, then hair piece D, folding under bottom seam allowance. Add pieces E and F.

5. Cut a strip measuring 1¼″ × 2″ (3.4cm × 5.4cm) for upper sash; cut strip measuring 1¾″ × 2″ (4.6cm × 5.4cm) for lower sash; use Pattern G to cut

Materials

Assorted patterned fabrics for bag back, kimono, and sashes, total of ½ yd (50cm) or less

Fabric for lining, ¼ yd (25cm) or less

White cotton for face and neck, ⅛ yd (15cm) or less

Black cotton for hair, ⅛ yd (15cm) or less

2″ (5cm) decorative cord or ribbon

Two 23″ (58cm) decorative cords or drawstrings

Cotton/polyester batting

Sheet of stiff cardboard

Fine-tip markers or embroidery floss, black and pink

Patterns on pages 116–118. Use ¼″ (0.75cm) allowance for all seams.

Step 1

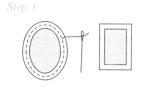

Step 2

Step 3

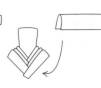

center kimono. Fold under and press all seam allowances. Overstitch top of upper sash to bottom of collar. Overstitch bottom of lower sash to top of G. Overstitch bottom of upper sash to top of lower sash.

6. Tie loose knot at center of 2″ (5cm) length of decorative cord or ribbon. Resulting piece should measure about 1½″ (4cm). Position at center of lower sash and stitch in place.

7. Using Pattern H, cut two sleeves, reversing pattern for one. Transfer markings. Cut two strips measuring ¾″ × 2½″ (2cm × 6.4cm) for sleeve top; cut two strips measuring 1½″ × 5½″ (4cm × 14cm) for bottom. Fold strips twice, lengthwise, then from end to end.

8. Attach sleeve tops and bottoms, blindstitching in position as shown and folding in raw edges on sleeves.

9. Fold in all raw edges, then blindstitch sleeves onto body.

10. Using Pattern I, cut back of bag, transferring fold line. Right sides together, stitch back to completed front, leaving top open. Turn right side out. Spread thin layer of batting evenly over inside of bag. Turn hems inward at fold line.

11. Fold each of two cords or drawstrings in half, marking center point with pin. Tuck and stitch one end of each in place onto turned-down hem of bag back, about ½″ (1.5cm) from top and ½″ (1.5cm) from side seam. Make Josephine knots at other ends (see page xix). Blindstitch in place on bag front, about ½″ (1.5cm) from top and ½″ (1.5cm) from side seam.

12. Using Pattern J, cut two for lining, transferring fold line. Right sides together, sew back and front lining together, leaving top open. Do not turn right side out. Fold and press top edge outward along fold line. Insert lining into bag. Adjust so that top edge of lining lies about ½″ (1.5cm) below top edge of bag and hides ends of cord. Pin in place and slip-stitch top edges together.

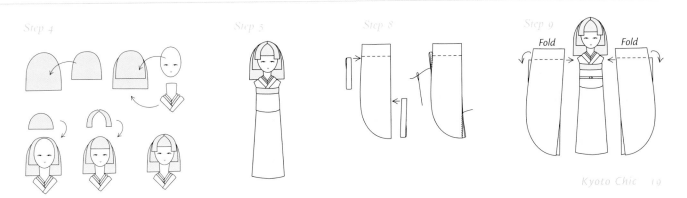

Step 4   Step 5   Step 8   Step 9   Fold   Fold

Conpaito

Whether you use it for candies, as its name suggests, as a purse, or for a string of pearls, colorful Conpaito *will remind you of the joy of summer and the laughter of friends.*

Materials

Solid dark fabric, ⅛ yd (15cm) or less

Solid light fabric, ⅛ yd (15cm) or less

Patterned fabric, ⅛ yd (15cm) or less

Fabric for lining, ¼ yd (25cm) or less

Embroidery floss

Two 29″ (75cm) ribbons or drawstring

1. Using Pattern A and patterned fabric, cut nine. From a light fabric, cut eighteen squares, each measuring 2″ × 2″ (5.4cm × 5.4cm). Cut twenty-seven squares from dark fabric.

2. Right sides together, stitch piece A to a light square, as shown. Add four more squares, alternating dark and light to create unit shown. Repeat to complete nine units. Align top edges of A pieces, basting and then stitching units together.

3. Thread needle with embroidery floss. From inside, pull needle through at point 1. Make a single stitch and re-insert needle. Resurface at point 2. Pull thread tight to create a tuck in fabric and backstitch to hold. Resurface needle at point 3 and make a single stitch. Draw thread across and exit at point 4. Do not gather. Backstitch to hold. Resurface at point 5 making a single stitch and re-insert needle. Resurface at point 6. Pull thread tight and backstitch to hold. Knot off securely. Repeat for all nine units. Wrong side out, join first and last units, creating a cylinder-like shape. Turn right side out.

4. At light square at bottom of each unit, match circles as shown. Pin. Stitch seams to close bottom of bag.

5. At center top of all A pieces, make a ⅜″ (1cm) tuck. Pin and baste in place.

6. Cut a strip of fabric for lining, measuring 4″ × 15½″ (10cm × 39cm). Right sides together, fold in half lengthwise and stitch seam. Baste along bottom edge and pull thread tight to gather. Backstitch to hold. Wrong sides together, position lining inside bag. Pin and stitch in place around top edge, tucking as necessary to fit.

7. Cut two hem pieces measuring 1½″ × 7″ (4cm × 18cm). Follow directions for making hems on page xvi.

8. To create fabric beads, cut two squares of fabric measuring 2″ × 2″ (4cm × 4cm). Follow directions for Method 4 on page xviii.

Pattern on page 119. Use ¼" (0.75cm) allowance for all seams.

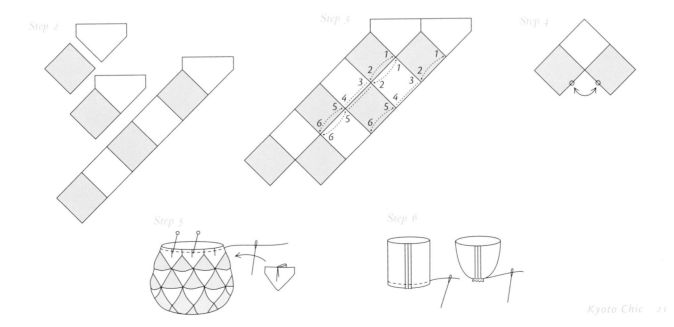

Step 2

Step 3

Step 4

Step 5

Step 6

Festival of Flowers

The flowers of Japan speak a silent language that whispers to us through our traditions, our legends, and our spirituality. A gift of flowers expresses so much more than kind thoughts or good wishes. Each flower has a meaning all its own, and there is an exquisite art to selecting blossoms for such occasions as the tea ceremony, festival days, or even the changing of the seasons.

When we celebrate flowers, we seek to purify the mind and heart and to find harmony with nature. There are flowers for every month of the year, and each represents a gift of the spirit. The primrose is the flower of youth, while the lotus promises immortality. The rose suggests fragility, and the imperial flower, the chrysanthemum, represents strength and courage. The achingly lovely cherry blossom—the darling flower of Japan and the symbol of the *samurai*—speaks of love and loyalty.

Each of the beautiful blossoms in these pages is cleverly crafted to hide a little pocket or pouch. Use them as the final touch to a beautifully wrapped present. Or make the flower itself your gift, tucking a note or a poem inside. Brighten the dinner table with a simple flower at each setting, and let each guest find tiny mints or colorful candies when the petals are parted.

Chinese Bellflower

*A delightful surprise atop a gift, turn the bellflower over to find a
hidden pocket, perfect for tiny trinkets.*

1. Using Pattern A, cut five small petal pieces. Wrong sides out, stitch first two
   petals together as shown. Add remaining three petals, joining last one to first.
   Finger press to open seams.

2. Cut a strip for center flower measuring 1″ × 3¼″ (2.8cm × 8.5cm). Wrong side
   out, fold in half and stitch ¼″ (0.75cm) from ends to make a loop. Stitch and
   gather along bottom, ¼″ (0.75cm) from edge. Turn right side out. Gather-stitch
   around top edge, but do not pull gathers yet.

3. Right sides together, insert center piece into flower. Adjust gathering stitches to
   fit. Pin and stitch in place. This forms front of flower.

4. Using Pattern B, cut five large petal pieces from a fabric that complements small
   petals. Stitch together as in Step 1. This forms back of flower.

5. Right sides together, place flower front on top of flower back. Sew together
   along perimeter of flower shape, as shown, leaving a 1″ (2.5cm) opening. Clip
   curves. Finger press seams. Turn flower right side out. Blindstitch opening closed.

Materials

Patterned fabrics for petals,
leaves, center flower, hem,
and bud, total of ¼ yd
(25cm) or less

Fabric for pocket lining,
⅛ yd (15cm) or less

Two 22″ (55cm) ribbons or
drawstrings

Cotton/polyester batting
for stuffing

Patterns on page 119. Use ¼″ (0.75cm) allowance for all seams.

Step 1   Step 2   Step 3

Step 5

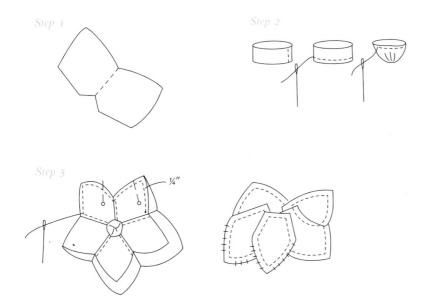

6. Cut strip measuring 2½" × 7½" (6.5cm × 19.4cm) for pocket lining. Sew ends together. Do not turn right side out. Fold in half and finger press gently to mark points A to D, as shown. Stitch once at each point and pull thread until points meet at center. Finger press gently to mark points E to H, as shown. Stitch once at each point and pull thread until points meet at center. Stitch to hold.

7. Position pocket lining inside flower. Pin and stitch in place along top edges.

8. Using Pattern C, cut six pieces from two complementary leaf fabrics. Place two leaf pieces—one from each fabric—right sides together. Sew around them, leaving ¾" (2cm) opening. Turn right side out. Blindstitch opening closed. Make a total of three leaves. Position leaf pieces at even intervals on flower back. Baste in place.

9. Cut two strips measuring 1½" × 4½" (4cm × 11.6cm) for hem. Follow directions for making hems on page xvi.

10. Using Pattern D, cut out two circles of fabric for beads. Follow directions for Method 5 on page xviii.

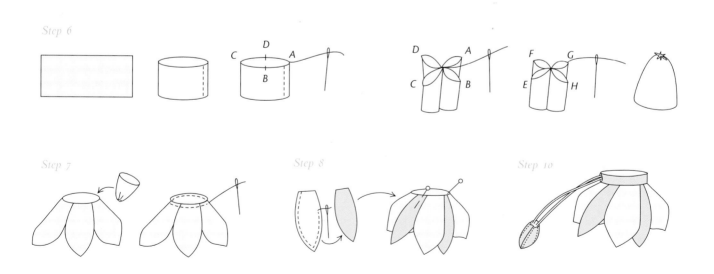

Step 6

Step 7

Step 8

Step 10

Chrysanthemum

Ah, chrysanthemum, the imperial flower of Japan! This lovely pochette *is perfect to hold a delicately scented kerchief.*

1. Cut two 9½″ × 9½″ (24.5cm × 24.5cm) squares, each from a different fabric. Right sides together, sew around them, leaving 1½″ (4cm) opening. Turn right side out. Blindstitch opening closed. Finger press seam.

2. Lay flat, with the fabric selected for the outside of the pouch facing up. Mark center points of each of four sides. Mark ¾″ (2cm) to left and right of all four marked center points. Lightly draw four lines linking these points, as shown.

3. Fold along marked lines to center as shown, creating petals. Pin and baste. Stitch petals ½″ (1.5cm) in from folds as shown. Do not stitch between petals. (This becomes a ribbon "loop.")

4. Fold back each petal point toward stitch line, approximately ⅛″ (0.4cm) away from it. Stitch to hold at each side of tip, about three stitches.

5. Insert both ribbons through all four loops. If you wish, add beads to end of each ribbon, knotting to hold in place. Pull ribbons to gather. Tie as desired.

Materials

Patterned fabric for outside pouch, ¼ yd (25cm)

Fabric for inside pouch, ¼ yd (25cm)

Two 15″ (38cm) ribbons or drawstrings

Four decorative beads, large enough to thread ribbons through easily

---

Use ¼″ (0.75cm) allowance for all seams.

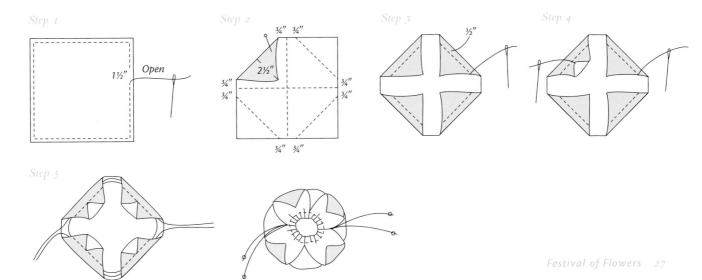

Step 1 — 1½″ — Open

Step 2 — ¾″ ¾″ — 2½″ — ¾″ ¾″ — ¾″ ¾″ — ¾″ ¾″

Step 3 — ½″

Step 4

Step 5

Camellia

This exquisite winter bloom, Camellia japonica, *is a reminder that beauty is as fleeting as footsteps in the snow. Picture this tiny purse dangling from the dainty wrist of a lady dressed in a kimono on her way to a secret tryst. In its hidden pocket, she keeps a love note . . .*

1. Cut two strips measuring 2¾″ × 7½″ (7.2cm × 19.4cm), one for outer pocket and one for pocket lining. Turn bottom under by ¼″ (0.75cm) and hem. Sew ends of outer pocket together and turn right side out.

2. Fold in half and finger press gently to mark points A to D, as shown. Stitch once at each point and pull thread tight until points meet at center. Finger press gently to mark points E to H, as shown. Stitch once at each point and pull thread tight until points meet at center. Stitch to hold.

3. Prepare pocket lining in same way as pocket, following Steps 1 and 2. Insert lining into pocket and baste in place, ¼″ (0.75cm) from top.

4. Turn pocket right side out. On outside, stitch a star with two strands of embroidery floss, double threaded in needle.

5. Using Pattern A, cut ten petal pieces. Select two petals. Right sides together, sew around them, leaving top open. Clip curves, then turn right side out. Finger press seam. Make a total of five petals.

Materials

Assorted patterned fabrics for petals, leaves, and outer pocket, ¼ yd (25cm) or less

Fabric for pocket lining, ⅛ yd (15cm) or less

Two 12″ (30cm) ribbons or drawstrings

Embroidery floss

Patterns on page 120. Use ¼″ (0.75cm) allowance for all seams.

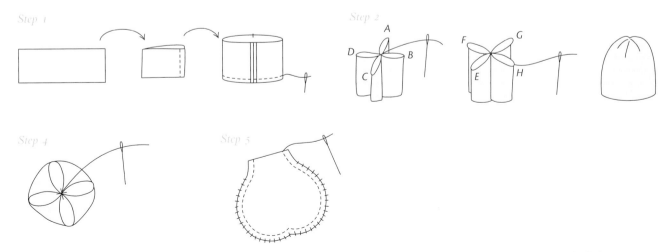

Step 1

Step 2

Step 4

Step 5

6. Stitch first petal onto right side of completed pocket. Add second petal, overlapping first by about ¼″ (0.75cm). To secure, stitch first petal to second at overlap, about ⅜″ (1cm) from top. Add third, fourth, and fifth petals around pocket in same way, forming completed flower.

7. Using Pattern B, cut six leaves from two complementary fabrics. Right sides together, sew around them, leaving top open. Clip curves, then turn right side out. Finger press seam. Repeat to complete three leaves.

8. Arrange leaves as desired and backstitch onto top of petals, sewing through petals, pocket, and pocket lining. Remove basting stitches from Step 3.

9. Cut two strips of fabric measuring 1½″ × 4½″ (4cm × 11.6cm) for hems. Follow directions for making hems on page xvi.

Step 6

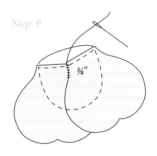

Step 7

Step 8

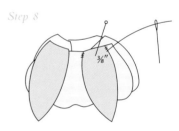

Step 9

Daffodil

This dainty daffodil or pretty trillium pouch brings a promise of spring as its blossoms peek through the snow.

1. Using Pattern A, cut two from complementary fabrics. Right sides together, stitch along seam lines, leaving a 1″ (2.5cm) opening. Turn right side out. Blindstitch opening closed.
2. Fold and pin each triangle point inward by 1½″ (4cm). Stitch across triangle point, ½″ (1.5cm) in from fold line, to complete three petals.
3. Turn wrong side out. Fold in half, matching points A. Stitch as shown, leaving ½″ (1.5cm) unstitched. Repeat, matching points B, and again, matching points C. Turn right side out.
4. Insert two ribbons or drawstrings, threading each through all three petals. Add beads to ends and knot together. Pull and tie as desired.

Materials

Patterned fabric for flower, ¼ yd (25cm) or less

Fabric for petals, ⅛ yd (15cm) or less

Two 16″ (40cm) ribbons or drawstrings

Two decorative beads, large enough to thread ribbons through easily

Pattern on page 121. Use ¼″ (0.75cm) allowance for all seams.

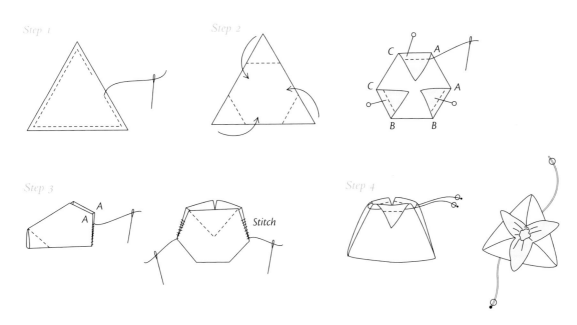

Step 1

Step 2

Step 3

Stitch

Step 4

Cosmos

*This tiny purse, held in the hand or tied lightly around the wrist,
sets off any evening gown to perfection!*

1. Using Pattern A, cut twelve petals from patterned fabric and twelve from complementary fabric. Match pairs, right sides together, and stitch around shape, leaving 1″ (2.5cm) opening. Turn right side out. Blindstitch opening closed. Finger press seam.

2. Using Pattern B, cut two for outer bag from patterned fabric and two for lining from complementary solid. Transfer marking to outer bag pieces. Using Pattern C, cut two center pieces. Fold under and finger press seam allowances on center pieces and appliqué in place onto outer bag pieces.

3. Right sides together, stitch curved sides of outer bag, leaving top open. Turn right side out.

4. Position, pin, and baste ten petals onto bag. Run a line of decorative stitching or *sashiko* stitching up the center of each petal, stopping 1½″ (4cm) up from bottom tip. Where petals touch, about 1¼″ (3.2cm) from bottom, stitch twice to hold neighboring petals together.

5. Right sides together, stitch sides of lining, leaving top open. Pin lining in place inside bag.

6. Cut two strips of fabric measuring 1½″ × 5½″ (4cm × 14.5cm) for hems. Follow directions for making hems on page xvi.

7. Fold each of two remaining petals in half lengthwise. Slide fabric until one curved edge overlaps the other slightly. Thread knot at end of ribbon through bottom tip of petal, hiding knot. Stitch edges of petal together from tip for about 1″ (2.5cm). Add two more stitches about ½″ (1.5cm) farther up.

Materials

Assorted patterned fabrics
for outer pocket, ⅛ yd
(15cm) or less

Fabric for lining, ⅛ yd (15cm)
or less

Two 29″ (75cm) ribbons or
drawstrings

Patterns on page 120. Use ¼″ (0.75cm) allowance for all seams.

Step 1

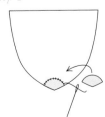

Step 2

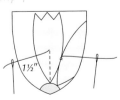

Step 4

1½″

Step 7

Sakura

This pretty pouch, a gift in itself, makes a wonderful party favor for a spring picnic. Tuck a tiny bottle of scent inside. The cherry motif brings good luck—it symbolizes beauty and the promise of spring.

1. Using Pattern A, cut ten petal pieces from complementary fabrics. Select two petals. Right sides together, sew around them, leaving a 1″ (2.5cm) opening. Clip curves, then turn right side out. Blindstitch opening closed. Finger press seam. Make five petals.

2. Overlap two petals by about 1″ (2.5cm). Stitch along overlap, about 1½″ (4cm). Add third, fourth, and fifth petals in same way, forming completed flower.

3. Cut two strips measuring 2″ × 7¼″ (5cm × 18.6cm), one from patterned fabric for pocket and one from lining fabric. Sew ends of pocket together and turn right side out. Turn bottom under by ¼″ (0.75cm) and hem.

4. Sew hemmed bottom of pocket to underside of petals.

5. Sew ends of pocket lining together. Do not turn right side out. Fold in half and finger press gently to mark points A to D, as shown. Stitch once at each point

Materials

Assorted patterned fabrics for petals, leaves, and outer pocket, total of ¼ yd (25cm)

Fabric for pocket lining

Two 25″ (60cm) ribbons or drawstrings

Patterns on page 123. Use ¼″ (0.75cm) allowance for all seams.

Step 1

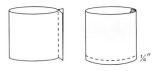

Step 2

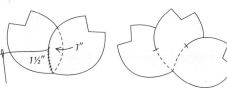

Step 3

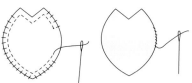

Step 4

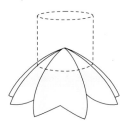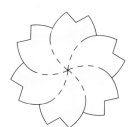

and pull thread until points meet at center. Finger press gently to mark points E to H, as shown. Stitch once at each point and pull thread until points meet at center. Stitch to hold.

6. Insert lining into pocket and pin in place.

7. Using Pattern B, cut six leaves. Right sides together, sew around them, leaving top open. Clip curves, then turn right side out. Finger press seam. Make a total of three leaves.

8. Arrange leaves as desired and backstitch onto top of pocket, sewing through both pocket and pinned pocket lining. Remove pins.

9. Cut two strips measuring 1½" × 4" (4cm × 10.6cm) for hems. Follow directions for making hems on page xvi.

10. Knot ribbons or drawstrings together at loose ends. Pull and tie as desired.

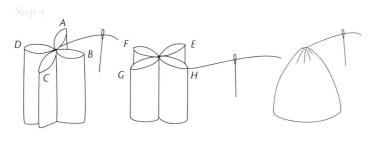

Step 5

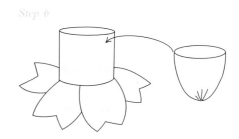

Step 6

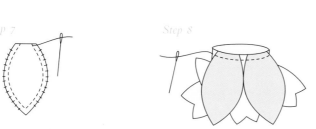

Step 7   Step 8

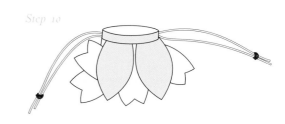

Step 10

Avalanche Lily

A symbol of purity, this lovely lily pouch is the perfect place to keep a simple strand of pearls.

1. Using Pattern A, cut star from patterned fabric. Clip all five inner angles on star as close as possible into seam allowance. For petals, cut five using Pattern B from a complementary fabric.

2. Right sides together, match each petal point to each of star's inner angles. Pin. Match dotted lines on each petal to dotted lines marked on stars, as shown. Baste, then stitch to create outer bag. Turn right side out.

3. Cut strip measuring 3″ × 8″ (7.8cm × 20.5cm) for pocket. Sew ends together. Do not turn right side out. Fold in half and finger press gently to mark points A to D, as shown. Stitch once at each point and pull thread until points meet at center. Finger press gently to mark points E to H, as shown. Stitch once at each point and pull thread until points meet at center. Stitch to hold. Turn bottom under by ¼″ (0.75cm) and hem. Place pocket lining, wrong side out, inside outer bag. Pin.

4. Cut two strips measuring 1½″ × 5″ (4cm × 13cm) for hems. Follow directions for making hems on page xvi.

5. Add beads to ends of ribbons or drawstrings and knot. Pull and tie as desired.

Materials

Assorted patterned fabrics for petals and outer pocket, ¼ yd (25cm)

Fabric for pocket lining, ⅛ yd (15cm)

Two 16″ (40cm) ribbons or drawstrings

Two beads

Patterns on page 122. Use ¼″ (0.75cm) allowance for all seams.

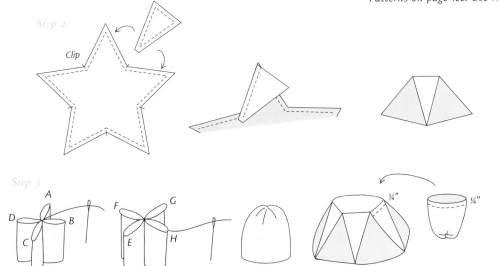

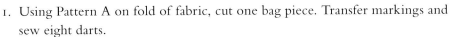

Double Petal Sakura

There are few scenes as enchanting as children in kimonos at play in a cherry grove as they welcome the spring. Their mother might take a bag like this with her to a cherry-viewing party, using it to gather the fallen blossoms and enjoy their short, sweet life.

1. Using Pattern A on fold of fabric, cut one bag piece. Transfer markings and sew eight darts.

2. Using Pattern B, cut nine petals. Fold in and baste seam allowance. Pin eight petals in position on bag, saving one petal to overlap seam when sides of bag will be sewn together. Appliqué eight petals in place. Right sides together, stitch side seam of bag. Turn right side out. Appliqué remaining petal over seamline.

3. Using Pattern C, cut bottom circle. Right sides together, pin and then stitch to bag. Turn right side out.

4. Using Patterns A and C, cut inner bag from lining fabric. Join side seams of A. Wrong sides together, pin and then stitch lining bottom to inner bag. Place

Materials

Assorted patterned fabrics
for petals, outer bag,
bottom bag, beads, and
leaves, ¼ yd (25cm)
Fabric for pocket lining,
⅛ yd (15cm)
Two 29" (75cm) ribbons or
drawstrings

Patterns on pages 123–125. Use ¼" (0.75cm) allowance for all seams.

Step 2

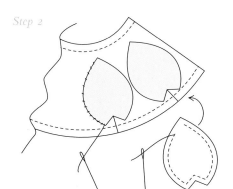

Step 4

lining inside bag. Fold and press top edges of both bag and lining inward to hide raw edges. Press. Blindstitch edges together along fold.

5. Using Pattern D, cut eighteen petals, nine each from two complementary fabrics. Right sides together, sew pairs together, leaving ¾″ (2cm) opening. Turn right side out. Blindstitch opening closed. Fold petal top down along fold line. Stitch in place, ⅜″ (1cm) below fold.

6. Sew continuously, without breaking thread, ⅜″ (1cm) from folded line to link all nine petals side by side in a loop. Backstitch to secure. Pin loop of petals at top of bag. Stitch in place along same stitchline used to create petal loop. Insert two ribbons or drawstrings, threading both through both sides of tube created at fold in petals. Knot ends.

7. To create fabric beads, cut two squares of fabric measuring 2″ × 2″ (5.4cm × 5.4cm). Follow directions for Method 1 on page xvii.

8. To add leaves to beads, use Pattern E to cut four leaf pieces. Right sides together, sew two pieces together, leaving opening. Turn right side out. Blindstitch opening closed. Stitch across center, pulling stitches to gather. Attach to bead at gathers.

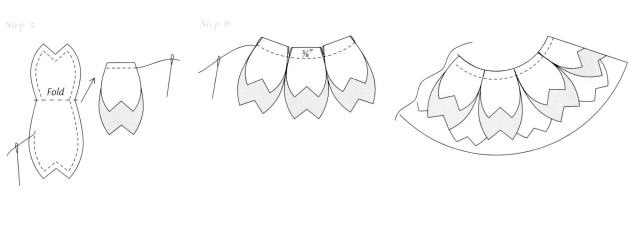

Step 5 *Step 6*

Step 8

Good Luck Dolls

One of the most charming of festival days in Japan is Girl's Day or Hina Matsuri. On March 3 each year, my mother would invite my little friends to see the wonderful array of dolls that she and I had collected. Prettily dressed in kimonos and tottering on tiny wooden clogs, we would admire the glorious costumes of the emperor and empress. The exquisite details of the dolls in their miniature courts, complete with tiny tea trays, chests, and even sewing boxes, would delight us. My mother would decorate the room with flowering plum blossoms, and this celebration was our way to greet spring.

In Japan, a girl's first gift from her grandmother is a doll—and that doll stays in the family even after she marries. There is a long tradition of using dolls to bring good luck and to protect against evil. In some regions, dolls that girls have outgrown are floated down the river in wooden boats, as a way of releasing the dolls' spirits and giving thanks for the health and happiness of the children who loved them. A certain kind of clay doll— *nagashi bina*—is made to attract the ill will that would otherwise befall people. These poor creatures are cast into the river, and the evil they have absorbed drowns with them.

When given as gifts, the dolls I have designed here bring nothing but goodwill and warm thoughts.

Village Girl

Sweet and simple, Village Girl *makes a pretty gift. The pouch is big enough to hold a comb, a compact, a handkerchief, or other party essentials.* Village Girl *also makes a lovely change purse.*

1. Using Pattern A, cut two. Choose plain white cotton for first piece (face) and patterned fabric for second (back hair). Transfer dotted lines onto face. Lightly draw or embroider features onto face.

2. Right sides together, stitch face to back hair, leaving bottom open. Turn right side out.

3. Using Pattern B, cut front hair. Right sides together, stitch front and back hair together along outer edge. Clip curve and turn right side out.

4. On hair front, clip inner curve. Turn under seam allowance and use zigzag or other patterned stitch along entire curve.

5. Blindstitch front hair in place onto face. Stuff with batting through opening at bottom. Baste bottom edges together.

6. Cut three strips of different patterned fabrics on bias for collars, measuring 1¼″ × 6″ (3.2cm × 16cm). Fold in half lengthwise, right side out.

7. Beginning at front left, stitch top collar piece along fold to left chin line (indicated by dotted lines on Pattern A), around back of hair, and to front chin line.

Patterns on pages 127–129. Use ¼″ (0.75cm) allowance for all seams.

Materials

Patterned fabric for dress, ⅛ yd (15cm) or less

Patterned fabrics for collars, hem, and hair, scraps

White cotton for face, scrap

Cotton/polyester batting, scraps

Fine-tip markers or embroidery floss, black and pink

Two 22″ (55cm) ribbons or drawstrings

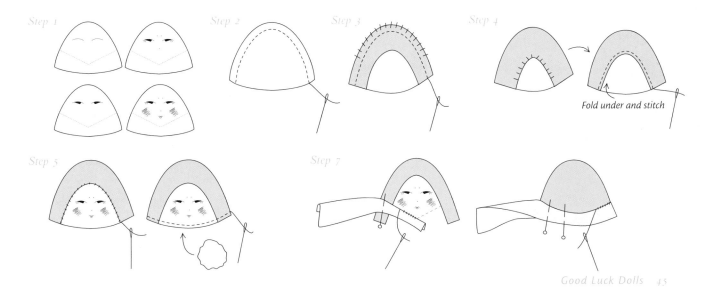

Step 1   Step 2   Step 3   Step 4

Fold under and stitch

Step 5   Step 7

8. Positioning ⅛″ (0.4cm) away from first stitch line, add middle and bottom collar pieces in same way, overlapping at front.

9. Using Patterns C and D, cut front and back dress. Right sides together, align at bottom and stitch side seams. Clip curves.

10. Using Pattern E, cut two for dress lining. Right sides together, stitch side seams and along top edge.

11. With dress front facing up, position lining on top of dress, aligning bottom edges. Both pieces are still wrong side out. Baste together *outside* seam lines, as shown. Turn right sides out.

12. Fold in seam allowance along top edge of dress front and back, clipping seam as necessary to make dress lie flat. Position head and collar inside dress. Pin in place and stitch. Baste lining to dress at bottom.

13. Cut two strips measuring 1½″ × 6″ (4cm × 15.5cm) for hems. Follow directions for making hems on page xvi.

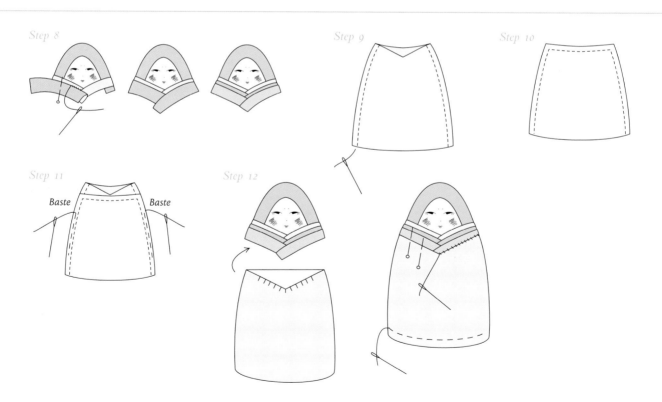

Step 8

Step 9

Step 10

Step 11

Baste   Baste

Step 12

Raindrop

These tiny Raindrop *dolls make lovely party favors, especially when they are filled with mints or candies.*

1. Using Pattern A, cut two from complementary fabrics, one for outer pouch and one for pouch lining. Fold outer pouch piece in half from A to B, with wrong side out. Stitch as shown. Repeat for pouch lining.

2. Turn outer pouch right side out, opening as shown. Position lining inside pouch, wrong sides together. Pin and baste lining to pouch along upper edges.

3. Cut two strips measuring 1½″ × 5½″ (4cm × 14.5cm) for hems. Follow steps 1 to 4 of making hems on page xvi.

4. Using Pattern B, cut five flower petals. Wrong side out, fold each three times as shown. Gather-stitch top edge.

5. With seam at back, position petals on front of pouch, over hem line. Stitch.

6. Using Pattern C, cut doll face from white cotton. Gather-stitch around seam allowance. Stuff with batting, gently pulling gathering stitches until face is 1″ (2.5cm) in diameter. Backstitch to hold. Lightly draw or embroider hair, eyes, nose, and mouth onto face.

7. Stitch completed face at center of petals. Pull ribbon or drawstring through opening in hem. Knot ends. Tie as desired.

Materials

Patterned fabric for outer pouch, ⅛ yd (15cm) or less

Fabric for pouch lining, ⅛ yd (15cm) or less

White cotton for face, scrap

Cotton/polyester batting, scraps

Fine-tip markers or embroidery floss, black and pink

23″ (58cm) ribbon or drawstring

Patterns on page 126. Use ¼″ (0.75cm) allowance for all seams.

Step 1

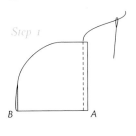

Step 2

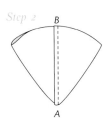
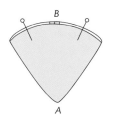

Step 4

Step 5

Step 6

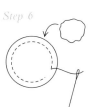

Step 7

Boy Acrobat

This playful pocket doll was inspired by Shi-Shi, *a lion from Chinese legend who was known for his bravery. Tie the* Boy Acrobat *to your child's backpack and let* Shi-Shi *take care of his latchkey.*

1. Cut strip measuring 3" × 7" (7.8cm × 18cm) for skirt. Right sides together, fold in half lengthwise and stitch side seam. Turn right side out. Gather lower edge until it measures 2¼" (5.8cm). Backstitch to hold. Center seam at back.

2. Cut strip measuring 1¾" × 5" (4.6cm × 13cm) for torso. Right sides together, fold in half lengthwise and stitch side seam. Turn right side out. Center seam at back.

3. Using Pattern A, cut two sleeve pieces. Right sides together, fold in half lengthwise and stitch side seam. Turn right side out. Center seam at back.

4. Using Pattern B, cut two hand pieces from white cotton. Fold in half twice and baste across top. Right sides together, pin hand to narrow edge of sleeve, folding raw edge under. Stitch in place through all layers. Right sides together, position sleeves on front of torso piece. Pin and then stitch in place through front layer of torso piece only. Turn right side out and press.

5. Cut strip measuring 1¼" × 5½" (3.2cm × 14cm) for belt. Fold in long edges lengthwise so that they meet. Fold under short edges by ¼" (0.75cm). Press. Right sides together, blindstitch one long edge to gathered edge of skirt. Turn right side out. Blindstitch other long edge to torso. Blindstitch short edges together.

Materials

Patterned fabrics for skirt, ⅛ yd (15cm) or less

Variety of patterned fabrics for torso, belt, hem, sleeves, helmet, and dragon tongue, scraps

White cotton for hands and face, scraps

Fabric for pocket lining, ⅛ yd (15cm) or less

Cotton/polyester batting, scraps

Fine-tip marker, black

Red crayon

Embroidery floss

Two 16" (40cm) ribbons or drawstrings

6" (15cm) cord or patterned string

Patterns on page 131. Use ¼" (0.75cm) allowance for all seams.

Step 1
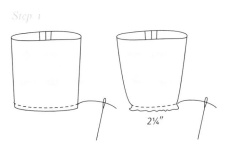

2¼"

Step 3
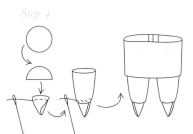

Step 4

Step 5
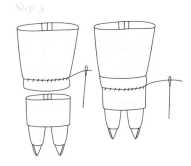

6. From lining fabric, cut strip measuring 3″ × 7″ (7.8cm × 18cm). Right sides together, fold in half end to end and stitch side seam. Gather-stitch along bottom edge and pull thread tight. Backstitch to hold. Wrong sides together, position lining inside skirt. Pin and stitch in place around top edge, tucking as necessary to fit.

7. Cut two strips measuring 2″ × 4½″ (5.4cm × 11.5cm) for hems. Follow directions on page xvi for making hems.

8. Using Pattern C, cut two face pieces from white cotton. Right sides together, stitch around seam allowance, leaving ¾″ (2cm) opening. Turn right side out. With fine-tip marker, lightly draw eyes onto face. Embroider mouth with red floss. Use red crayon to add a little color to cheeks. Stuff face with batting. Blindstitch opening closed.

9. Using Pattern D, cut helmet. Right sides together, fold in half lengthwise and stitch side seam. Turn right side out. Center seam at back.

10. Using Pattern E, cut four ear pieces from two complementary fabrics. Match pairs. Right sides together, stitch side seams, leaving curved edge open. Turn right side out. Fold twice as shown. Baste bottom edge. Stitch to top of helmet as shown. Fold under bottom edge of helmet by ½″ (1.5cm). Press. Use a decorative stitch to hold in place.

11. Using Pattern F, cut one dragon tongue (no seam allowance). Fold in half, right side out, and stitch as shown. Make a tuck-fold across helmet, about ⅜″ (1cm) from bottom. Insert raw edges of tongue in fold. Stitch in place. To create dragon eyes, embroider using contrasting floss to right and left above tongue.

12. Take a 6″ (15cm) cord or decorative string. Knot twice at center and once at each end. Stitch in place around face.

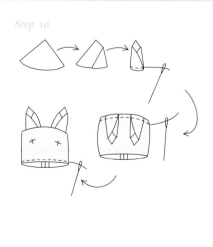

Step 6

Step 8

Step 10

Step 11

Step 12

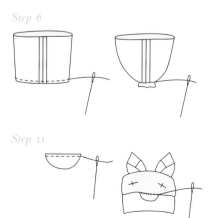

Pretty Princess

Perfect to use as a paperweight, this Pretty
Princess *will brighten any desk or writing table.*

1. Using Pattern A, cut doll face from plain white cotton. Gather-stitch around seam allowance. Stuff batting inside face, gently pulling gathering stitches until the face is about 1″ (2.5cm) in diameter. Backstitch to hold.

2. With fine-tip marker, lightly draw hair, eyes, nose, and mouth. Alternatively, embroider features onto face.

3. Cut strip measuring 4¼″ × 7½″ (11cm × 19.4cm) for dress. Fold in half end to end with right sides together and stitch seam. Gather-stitch dress bottom. Pull stitches tight and backstitch to hold. Turn right side out.

4. Turn under and hem top edge, leaving 2″ (5cm) opening across back seam line. Stitch top of doll face into opening.

5. Pin dress to sides of face. Stitch three or four times to hold.

6. Stuff dried beans, peas, or lentils into opening to weight down dress. Gather-stitch opening and pull tight to close. Backstitch to hold. Stitch dress around chin. Make two bows from ribbon and stitch to front of dress.

Materials

Patterned fabric for dress, ⅛ yd (15cm) or less

Plain white cotton for face, scrap

Cotton/polyester batting, scraps

Fine-tip markers or embroidery floss, black and pink

Two tablespoons dried peas, beans, or lentils

Two 12″ (30cm) ribbons

Pattern on page 129. Use ¼″ (0.75cm) allowance for all seams.

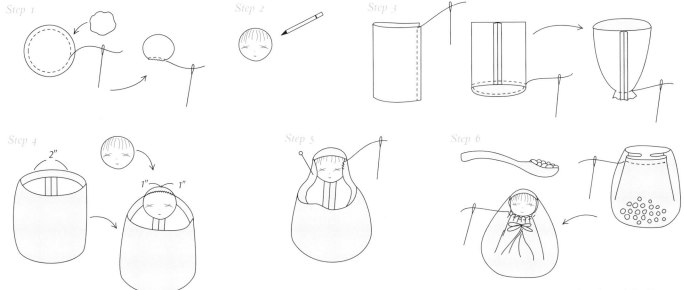

Step 1   Step 2   Step 3

Step 4   Step 5   Step 6

Playtime!

This colorful pincushion can double as a paperweight—or as an unusual ornament. You can also make a slightly larger doll, without the cushion, to use as the finishing touch to an elegantly wrapped gift.

Materials

11″ (28cm) circumference/3″ (7.6cm) diameter Styrofoam ball (available in this size or similar sizes from craft stores)

Sheet of cardboard

Patterned fabric for ball, base, and doll body, ½ yd (50cm) or less

Cotton/polyester batting

White cotton for heads, scraps

Fine-tip marker, black

Colored pencil, red

Craft glue

Heavy-duty thread or embroidery floss

(continued on facing page)

1. Prepare Styrofoam ball by slicing in half with craft knife. Using Pattern A, cut one (no seam allowance). Gather around circumference, wrapping Styrofoam inside, and pull stitches tight. Backstitch to hold.

2. Using Pattern B, cut one from cardboard (no seam allowance) and one from fabric (add seam allowance). Gather around circumference, wrapping cardboard inside, and pull stitches tight. Backstitch to hold. Wrong sides together, pin in place onto base of covered Styrofoam. Blindstitch in place.

3. With 20″ (50cm) decorative cord, make two Josephine knots, one above the other (see page xix). Curl ends of cord as shown. Glue in position onto covered Styrofoam.

4. Cut a strip measuring 3″ × 3½″ (7.8cm × 9cm) for body. On wrong side, mark points A to D as shown. Fold to match points A. Stitch along seam allowance. Repeat with next three corners, matching points B, C, and D. Turn right side out. Stuff through opening at tummy. For arms, use a large needle to push a little of fabric at tips to inside of doll. Stuff inside tummy until firm.

Patterns on page 130. Use ¼″ (0.75cm) allowance for all seams.

Step 1

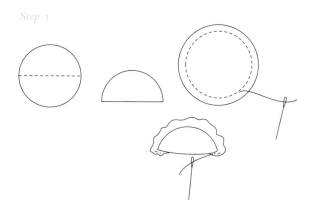

Step 2

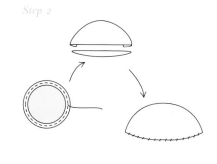

Step 3

5. Cut square measuring 2½″ × 2½″ (6.4cm × 6.4cm) for head. Put a wad of batting at center, pulling fabric around it to make head measuring about ¾″ (2cm) in diameter. Wrap with heavy-duty thread several times as shown. With fine-tip marker, lightly draw features onto head. Stuff tail into opening in body. Blindstitch opening closed.

6. Draw nine 7″ (18cm) strands of heavy-duty thread or embroidery floss through back of head. Braid for about 3½″ (9cm). Wrap and knot tightly with new thread to secure.

7. Repeat Steps 4 to 6 to make second doll. Position and blindstitch dolls in place on ball.

20″ (50cm) decorative cord

18″ (45cm) decorative cord (*Baby Doll with Fruit* variation)

Fabric scraps for fruit and leaves (*Baby Doll with Fruit* variation)

Fabric or ribbon for collar (*Baby Doll with Fruit* variation)

Embroidery floss, black (*Baby Doll with Fruit* variation)

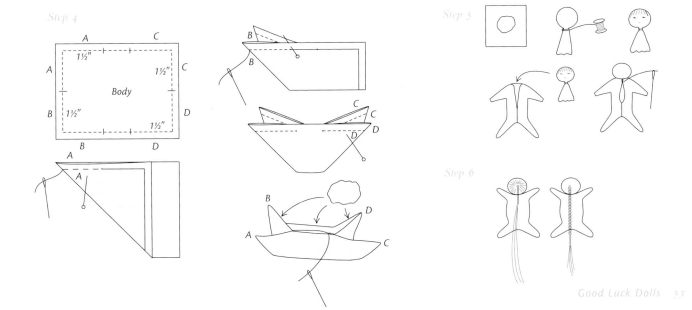

Variation 1—Baby Doll with Fruit

1. For pincushion decorated with strawberries, follow Steps 1 and 2 to prepare ball and Steps 4 to 6 to make one doll. To make fruit, cut one using Pattern C. Right sides together, fold in half lengthwise and sew bottom seam. Open out to create cone shape. Stitch side seam, leaving top open. Turn right side out. Gather-stitch top edge, stuffing with batting. Pull stitches tight to close. Backstitch to hold. Make three.

2. To make leaf and stem, cut a square measuring 1¼″ × 1¼″ (3.4cm × 3.4cm). Turn under seams by ⅛″ (0.4cm). Make one gathering stitch at the midpoint of each side. Pull tight and backstitch to hold. Make three. Stitch leaves to top of each fruit. Stitch bunch in position on ball. Decorate as shown with 18″ (45cm) decorative cord, rolling ends and gluing cord to ball.

Variation 1—Baby Doll with Fruit

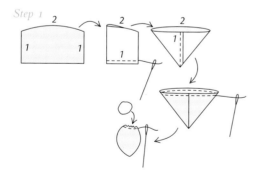

Step 1

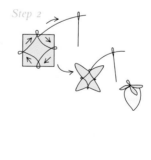

Step 2

1. To make slightly larger doll body, cut strip 3½″ × 4½″ (9cm × 11.5cm) for body and follow Step 4 on page 52. You can vary final shape of body by varying amount of stuffing in arms and legs. Blindstitch opening closed. Cut strip on bias, measuring 1¾″ × 4½″ (4.4cm × 11.4cm) for collar. Alternatively, use length of ribbon. Right sides together, fold in half to make a loop. Stitch edges together. Turn right side out and fold in half lengthwise. Stitch and gather raw edges. Pull to form a ½″ (2.5cm) diameter hole inside loop. Backstitch to hold.

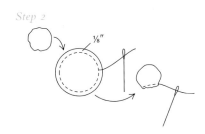

2. Using Pattern D, cut out face from white cotton. Stitch and gather around face piece along seam allowance. Stuff and pull gathering stitches closed. Backstitch to hold. Using black, fine-tip marker, lightly draw eyes, nose, and eyebrows. Add lips, mouth, and cheeks with red pencil. With black embroidery floss, stitch several short lines for hair.

3. Position head within collar and stitch in place. Attach collar and head to body above arms.

Variation 2—Baby Doll

Step 1

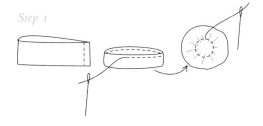

Step 2

⅛″

Step 3

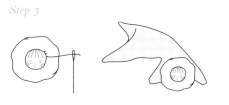

Pocket Baby

In Japan, this hai-hai *doll is a gift to celebrate a new birth. Use this tiny doll to decorate a baby shower gift. Tuck a note inside, wishing the newborn health, happiness, and good fortune.*

1. Using Pattern A, cut one on fold, transferring markings. Wrong side out, fold in half along fold line. Stitch along dotted lines as shown, leaving neckline, train, top, and sleeves open. Baste pleats. Turn right side out.

2. Cut four strips measuring 1″ × 2″ (2.5cm × 5cm); two are for outer sleeves and two for inner sleeves. Right sides together, join shorter sides of each outer sleeve to make two loops. Turn right side out and fold lengthwise. Pin to hold. Fold each inner sleeve in half from end to end. Fold lengthwise. Pin to hold. Position inside outer sleeve, with folded edge showing. Pin and stitch in place. Repeat for second sleeve.

3. Turn under raw edges of sleeve holes on body piece A. Insert sleeves and stitch in place.

4. To create trim, cut a strip measuring 1½″ × 6½″ (4cm × 16.5cm) and another measuring 1½″ × 6″ (4cm × 15cm). Right sides together, join short edges of longer strip to make loop. Turn right side out and fold lengthwise. Pin to hold. Fold shorter strip in half from end to end. Fold lengthwise. Pin to hold. Position

Materials

Patterned fabrics for body, ¼ yd (25cm) or less

Scraps for sleeves, bottom trim, and bib

White cotton for face, scrap

Fabric for inner pocket, ⅛ yd (15cm) or less

Cotton/polyester batting, scraps

Fine-tip marker, black

Embroidery floss, red

Two 16″ (40cm) ribbons or drawstrings

Patterns on pages 131–132. Use ¼″ (0.75cm) allowance for all seams.

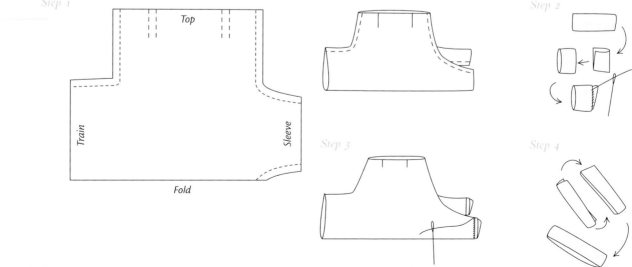

Step 1

Top

Train

Sleeve

Fold

Step 2

Step 3

Step 4

short strip inside long strip, with folded edge showing. Pin and stitch in place.

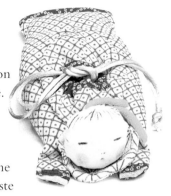

5. Turn under raw edge of train opening on body piece A. Position trim inside opening so that both layers show, and stitch in place. Stuff body and sleeves evenly with batting through neckline opening.

6. Cut two strips measuring 3″ × 4¼″ (7.8cm × 11cm) for inner pocket. Right sides together, stitch along three sides, leaving one longer side open at top. Position pocket inside stuffed body. Baste and then stitch in place.

7. Cut two strips measuring 1½″ × 5″ (4cm × 13cm) for hem. Follow instructions for making hems on page xvi.

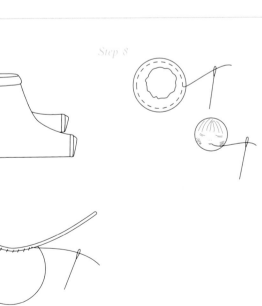

8. Using Pattern B, cut doll face from plain white cotton. Stitch and gather around seam allowance. Stuff batting inside face, gently pulling gathering stitches until face is about 2″ (5cm) in diameter. Backstitch to hold. With fine-tip marker, lightly draw hair, eyes, and nose. Make one or two small stitches with red embroidery thread for mouth. Alternatively, embroider all features onto face.

9. Using Pattern C, cut two bib pieces. Right sides together, stitch seams, leaving top open. Turn right side out. Cut strip of fabric measuring 1″ × 7½″ (2.8cm × 19.4cm). Fold in and stitch all seam allowances to hide raw edges. Position bib at center of strip and stitch. Tie bib around neckline.

Step 5

Step 7

Step 8

Step 9

Tea and Company

お茶の集い

The designs in these pages blend two traditions that are a part of women's lives: the making of tea and the joy of needlework. From early in the ninth century, when Zen priests returning from China introduced the medicinal values of tea leaves into Japan, tea has been a natural part of life. An invitation to tea has taken on meanings much deeper than those of a

simple social occasion. In a ceremony that is governed by age-old rituals, a bitter-tasting green tea, *maccha*, is offered in fine porcelain and in a setting of seasonal flowers. Guests' kimonos are also in tune with the seasons. The ceremony is a form of quiet meditation in which we take time to appreciate the connections between aesthetic beauty, the simple wonders of nature, and the cycles of the universe. Tea becomes a medicine for the mind and the soul.

The fabric arts are closely associated with the tea ceremony. Small pouches and other crafts are made from leftover scraps of fine silk and used to hold teapots and tea utensils. Elaborately tied with silk strings, the bags are decorated with butterflies, wisteria, or peach blossoms. Just as the purpose of the tea ceremony is to find harmony by pleasing the aesthetic senses, so the goal in needlework is to create something of beauty, stitched to perfection.

Little Teapot

Little Teapot *celebrates two arts for which Japanese women are famed—the eloquence of the tea ceremony and the intricacy of fine needlework. Use it as a kitchen ornament or as an unusual pincushion in your sewing room.*

1. Cut three circles from complementary fabrics. Increase accordingly if using slightly larger Styrofoam ball.
   Pot: 8½″ (21.8cm) diameter
   Lid: 3″ (7.8cm) diameter
   Lid knob: 2″ (5.4cm) diameter
2. Prepare Styrofoam ball by slicing off ⅝″ (1.8cm) from top and ⅜″ (1cm) from bottom.
3. Wrap ball with layer of batting. Secure by wrapping several times with lace tatting or dental floss.
4. Gather-stitch raw edge of pot fabric. Wrap around ball and pull stitches tight. Blindstitch tightly at top of ball.

Materials

Patterned fabrics for pot, knob, and lid, ¼ yd (25cm) or less

Knob, scrap

Felt for spout and handle, scraps

10½″ (27cm) circumference or similar size Styrofoam ball

Cotton/polyester batting

9½″ (24cm) ribbon or decorative cord

Craft glue

Lace tatting or dental floss

Stiff cardboard

Patterns on page 133. Use ¼″ (0.75cm) allowance for all seams.

Step 2

Cut ⅝″

Cut ⅜″

Step 3

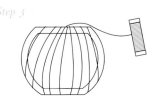

Step 4

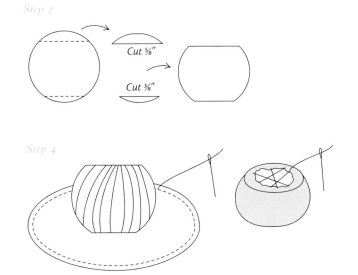

5. Cut a circle measuring 2½" (6.4cm) diameter from stiff cardboard. Glue onto lid fabric. Gather-stitch around edges of fabric circle. Pull tight and backstitch to hold. Gather-stitch around circumference of lid knob fabric. Stuff with batting until firm while pulling gathering stitches tight. Backstitch to hold. Sew knob to center top of lid.

6. Blindstitch lid in place on top of pot. Cover stitches with ribbon or cord.

7. Using Pattern A, cut spout from felt. Fold along center. Overcast-stitch long edge. Attach spout to front of pot, about ½" (1.5cm) from top.

8. Using Pattern B, cut handle from felt. Overcast-stitch lengthwise to create tube, leaving ¼" (0.75cm) open at each end. Open out ends and stitch to pot about ½" (1.5cm) from top.

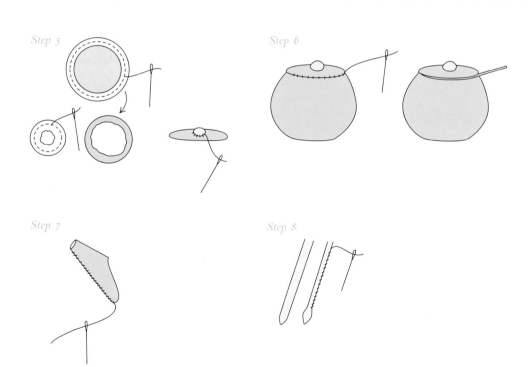

Step 5

Step 6

Step 7

Step 8

Sewing Box and Thimble

A charming gift for anyone who loves to sew, this little box is the perfect place for needles, bright threads, scissors, and snips. The handy cushion on the lid keeps pins safely in place. And the colorful thimble protects nimble fingers.

Sewing Box

1. Cut Pattern A from cardboard. Transfer all dotted lines. Wrong side up, score with craft knife so that cardboard folds along dotted lines.
2. Position cardboard Pattern A as desired onto fabric. Draw around entire piece, ⅜" (1cm) from all edges of cardboard. Cut fabric. At each corner, make ¼" (0.75cm) cuts as shown to allow corners to fold.
3. Reposition cardboard Pattern A onto fabric, making sure that ⅜" (1cm) allowance is still even. Glue carefully and fold evenly onto cardboard.
4. Cut four strips of cardboard measuring 2" × 3" (5cm × 7.6cm) for side panels. Mark dotted lines. Position on fabric, add ⅜" (1cm) allowance, and cut, as in Step 2. Glue and fold fabric onto cardboard panels, as in Step 3.
5. Cut four strips of cardboard measuring ⅜" × 1¾" (1cm × 4.4cm). Prepare as in Step 4. (These strips hold items inside box.)

Patterns on pages 133–134. Use ¼" (0.75cm) allowance for all seams.

Materials for Sewing Box

Sheet of light, sturdy cardboard

Patterned fabric for outside of box, ¼ yd (25cm) or less

Plain fabric for inside lining and pincushion, ⅛ yard (15cm) or less

Cotton/polyester batting

Craft glue

Cutting mat

Craft knife

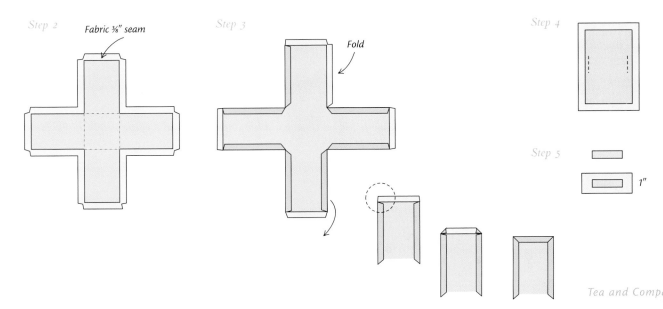

Step 2 — Fabric ⅜" seam

Step 3 — Fold

Step 4

Step 5 — 1"

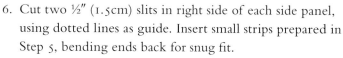

6. Cut two ½″ (1.5cm) slits in right side of each side panel, using dotted lines as guide. Insert small strips prepared in Step 5, bending ends back for snug fit.

7. Cut square measuring 2″ × 2″ (5cm × 5cm) from cardboard for base of box. Position on fabric, add allowances, and cut, as in Step 2.

8. Wrong sides together, glue side panels and base in place onto box A.

9. Cut Pattern B from cardboard. Transfer all dotted and solid lines. Wrong side up, score with craft knife so that cardboard folds along dotted lines. Cut completely through short solid lines at each corner of pattern. Fold along dotted lines. Glue four corners as shown.

10. Cut strip of fabric measuring 2¼″ × 9½″ (9.6 × 24cm). Place lid on top of fabric, centered horizontally and vertically. Trim corners of fabric so that they will neatly wrap around sides of lid. Glue fabric and wrap onto lid.

11. Cut square of fabric measuring 2⅛″ × 2⅛″ (5.4cm × 5.4cm). Glue to inside of lid.

12. To make pincushion, cut square of cardboard measuring 2⅛″ × 2⅛″ (5.4cm × 5.4cm). Cut square of fabric measuring 4″ × 4″ (10cm × 10cm). Carefully wrap edges of fabric around cardboard, stuffing with batting, and glue in place. Glue pincushion to top of lid.

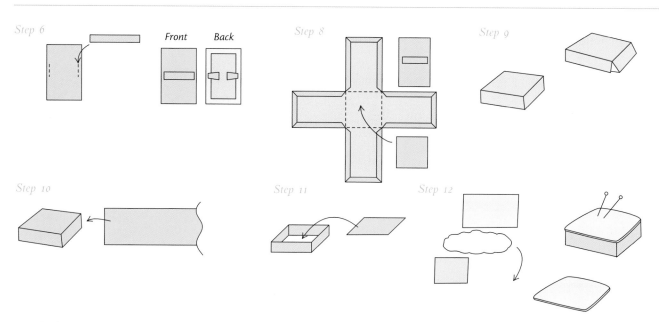

Step 6   Front   Back   Step 8   Step 9

Step 10   Step 11   Step 12

Thimble

1. Cut strip of interfacing measuring 2″ × 2½″ (5cm × 6.4cm). Fold lengthwise into thirds and baste to hold. Cut strip of fabric measuring 2¼″ × 3¼″ (5.6cm × 8.2cm). Place basted interfacing at center, turn in sides and top, and baste. Turn in bottom and blindstitch edge. Slip-stitch ends together firmly to form loop.

2. Make small stitches to mark four points at equal distance from each other around top of loop. Repeat around bottom of loop. With fine embroidery floss or silk thread, make small stitches from first point on top edge diagonally across to second point on bottom edge. Stitch diagonally up to next point on top edge. Repeat around loop, creating criss-cross pattern.

3. Divide top and bottom edges once more, making tiny stitches between four points made in Step 2. Change thread color and stitch diagonally from point to point, creating cross-hatch pattern. Change thread color again, and make final row of stitches lengthwise around center of thimble.

Materials for Thimble

Patterned fabric, scrap

Interfacing, scrap

Fine embroidery floss, three colors

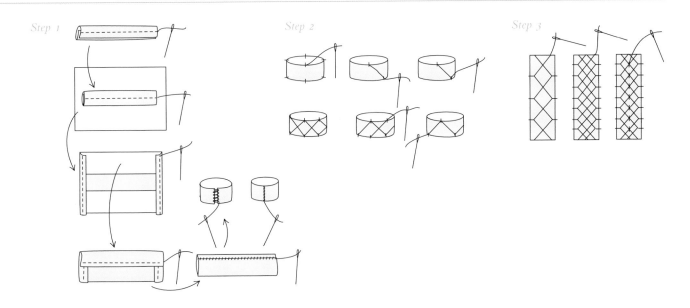

Step 1   *Step 2*   *Step 3*

Cherry Surprise

The dancing cherries on this pretty pincushion will brighten the winter days and turn your thoughts to the joys of spring. A perfect gift for anyone who sews!

1. Cut fourteen strips, seven from each of two complementary fabrics, measuring 1½″ × 3″ (4cm × 7.8cm). Mark center of each strip. Sew pairs together, one of each fabric, along one short edge to make seven pairs.

2. Matching center point of top fabric in first pair to top edge of second pair, sew all seven pairs together. Gather-stitch across all seven pairs, ¼″ (0.75cm) below top angles at which they join.

3. Taking care not to trap gathering stitches, join last pair to first pair as in Step 2, creating a tube. Fold raw edges inward at gather-stitch line. Pull gathering stitches tight, hiding raw edges. Backstitch to hold. Fold bottom raw edge under also, ¼″ (0.75cm) above bottom angles at which pairs join.

4. Cut strip of cardboard measuring ½″ × 9½″ (1.5cm × 24cm). Glue ends together, overlapping by ½″ (1.5cm) to make loop. Insert loop beneath folded-under edge at bottom. Stuff entire pincushion firmly with batting or fabric

Materials

Two fabrics for pincushion, ⅛ yd (15cm) each or less

Scraps for cherries

Scraps of green felt for leaves

Sheet of cardboard

Craft glue

Embroidery floss

Cotton/polyester batting or fabric scraps

Patterns on page 135. Use ¼″ (0.75cm) allowance for all seams.

Step 2

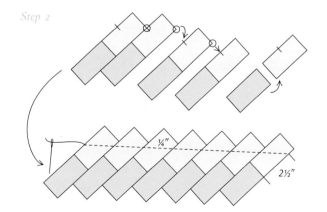

Step 3

scraps. Using Pattern A, cut one from cardboard (no seam allowance) and one from fabric (add seam allowance). Gather around circumference, wrapping cardboard inside, and pull stitches tight. Backstitch to hold. Wrong sides together, stitch in place around bottom edges of pincushion.

5. Using Pattern B, cut twelve cherries. Gather-stitch around circumference, stuffing with batting. Pull thread tight and backstitch to hold. Using Pattern C, cut twelve from felt. Stitch one to top of each cherry.

6. Cut twelve strands of embroidery floss, each measuring 4″ (10cm). Thread each through a leaf so that leaf sits at center point of strand. Gather loose strands and stitch. Position on top of pincushion, allowing leaves and cherries to fall evenly around it. Stitch to hold. Wrap ½″ (1.5cm) diameter button with fabric, gluing to hold. Sew or glue to top of pincushion, hiding earlier stitches and tips of embroidery floss.

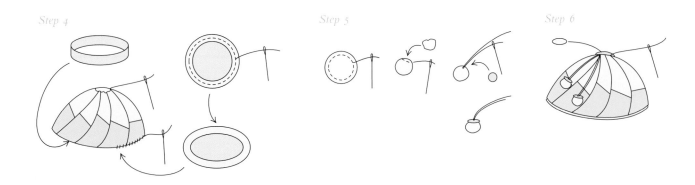

Step 4

Step 5

Step 6

Flower Box

Give Flower Box *as a gift, or keep it to hold your threads, scissors, and the pieces for your next quilt block. The top is reminiscent of a traditional patchwork quilt.*

1. For lid, cut strip of cardboard measuring 1¼″ × 18½″ (3.2cm × 47cm). With craft knife, score lengthwise, ½″ (1.5cm) from top edge. Make ½″ (1.5cm) clips all along top edge for easy folding. Glue ends, overlapping by ½″ (1.5cm) to make loop. Cut strip of fabric measuring 2″ × 18½″ (5cm × 47cm). Fold bottom edge under lengthwise by ¾″ (2cm). Insert unclipped edge of cardboard into fold line and glue fabric to both sides of card. Fabric should reach clips along top edge of card. Gently push clipped top edge of loop inward along score line.

2. Using Pattern A, cut one from cardboard (no seam allowance) and one from lining fabric (add seam allowance). For lid lining, gather-stitch around seam allowance, wrapping cardboard circle inside, and pull stitches tight. Backstitch to hold. Glue about ½″ (1.5cm) around outer edge of wrong side of wrapped circle. Position beneath loop and push up, attaching lid lining to turned-in clipped edge of loop. Press firmly until dry.

Materials

Large sheet of cardboard

Patterned fabric for outer box, bottom, and lid, ¼ yd (25cm) or less

Assortment of ten floral fabrics for lid, total of ⅛ yd (15cm) or less

Fabric for lining, ⅛ yd (15cm) or less

Craft glue

Patterns on pages 135–136. Use ¼″ (0.75cm) allowance for all seams.

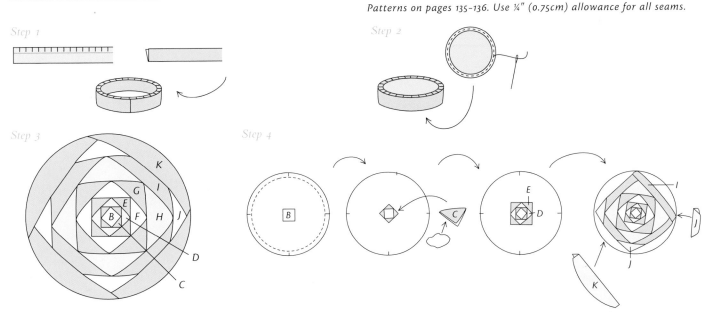

3. Cut variety of floral fabrics for lid top as follows, using photographs and diagram as guides.

> Cut one square B, measuring ¾″ × ¾″ (2cm × 2cm)
> Cut four square C, measuring ¾″ × ¾″ (2cm × 2cm)
> Cut four square D, measuring ¾″ × ¾″ (2cm × 2cm)
> Cut four square E, measuring 1″ × 1″ (2.5cm × 2.5cm)
> Cut four square F, measuring 1½″ × 1½″ (4cm × 4cm)
> Cut four square G, measuring 2″ × 2″ (5cm × 5cm)
> Cut four square H, measuring 2¼″ × 2¼″ (5.6cm × 5.6cm)
> Cut four rectangle I, measuring 1½″ × 3½″ (4cm × 9cm)
> Cut four using Pattern J
> Cut four using Pattern K

Right side out, fold shapes C to H in half diagonally to create triangles; fold I, J, and K in half lengthwise.

4. Glue shape B to center of lid top prepared in Step 2. Put a little light batting inside triangles C. Glue in place onto lid, overlapping raw edge of B. Repeat with pieces D to J, building lid outward. Put a little batting inside K and glue in place, using a toothpick to tuck raw edges neatly beneath fabric at sides of loop. Glue fabric securely in place. Allow to dry.

5. For outside of base, cut strip of cardboard measuring 2½″ × 18½″ (6.4cm × 47cm). With craft knife, score lengthwise, ½″ (1.5cm) from bottom edge. Make ½″ (1.5cm) clips all along bottom edge for easy folding. Glue ends, overlapping by ½″ (1.5cm), to make loop. Cut strip of fabric measuring 2½″ × 18½″ (6.4cm × 47cm). Fold top edge under lengthwise by ¼″ (.75cm). Insert cardboard into this fold line and glue fabric to both sides of card. Fabric should reach clips

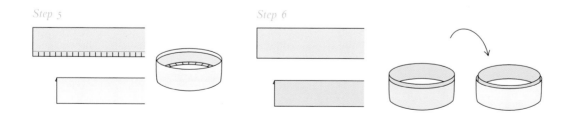

Step 5   Step 6

along bottom edge of card. Gently push clipped bottom edge of loop inward along score line.

6. For inside rim, cut a strip of cardboard measuring 2¼″ × 18½″ (5.6cm × 47cm). Glue ends, overlapping by ½″ (1.5cm), to make loop. Cut strip of fabric measuring 1½″ × 18½″ (4cm × 47cm). Glue over top edge of loop, wrapping so that about ⅜″ (1cm) is on outside, with remainder folded over to inside. Cut second strip of fabric for lining, measuring 1½″ × 18½″ (4cm × 47cm). Glue to inside of loop, so that top edge overlaps bottom edge of first fabric. Insert finished rim into base from Step 5.

7. Using Pattern A, cut two from cardboard (no seam allowance); cut one from patterned fabric and one from lining. Gather-stitch fabric around seam allowances, wrapping a cardboard circle inside each one, and pull stitches tight. Backstitch to hold. Glue about ½″ (1.5cm) around outer edge of wrong side of circle wrapped in lining fabric. Position above loop and push down, attaching bottom to base. Press firmly until dry. Glue circle wrapped in decorative fabric in place to form bottom of box.

Variation

It's easy to vary the pattern on the lid. Try making pieces B to H from hexagons instead of squares and see what happens!

Step 7

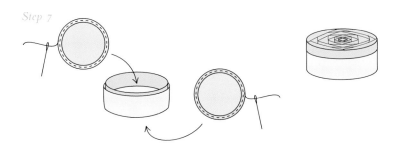

Eleganz

Similar to Oyster (page 16), the base of Eleganz is made from a seashell. It will take care of your pins and needles.

1. Position shell on a piece of fabric that is about one and a half times larger than it and cut around it. Gather-stitch around all edges. Smear glue around top outside and inside edges of shell and place inside gathered fabric. Pull gathering stitches tight, finger pressing lightly to stick to glue. Backstitch to hold. Shell should be covered evenly, with no puckers.

2. Using Pattern A, cut leaf. Right side out, fold in half and gather curved edge. Pull thread tight to close. Glue leaf to inside edge of shell as shown.

3. Using Pattern B, cut flower. (You may need to adjust size of circle if you are using larger or smaller shell.) Gather-stitch around edges. Stuff with batting until firm and pull stitches tight. Double-stitch to hold.

4. Secure decorative thread with doublestitch on back of flower piece. Draw thread around to front and secure at center. Repeat around entire flower until it is divided into about fourteen even sections. Glue flower securely inside shell, pressing in place for at least two minutes.

Materials

Small sea shell—
    shell photographed
    measures about 2″ × 2½″
    (5cm × 6.4cm)
Patterned fabric for shell
    cover, flower, and leaf,
    ⅛ yd (15cm) or less
Cotton/polyester batting
    (continued on following page)

Patterns on page 137. Use ¼″ (0.75cm) allowance for all seams.

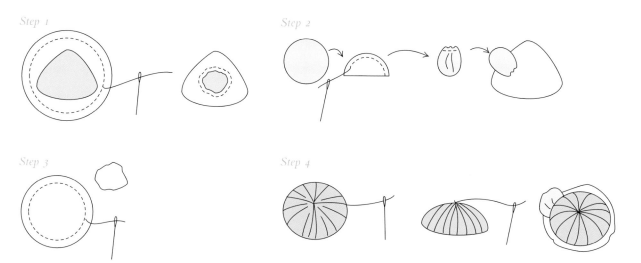

Step 1

Step 2

Step 3

Step 4

Variation

Prepare shell as in Step 1, but add two more leaves, following directions in Step 2. Prepare flower as in Steps 3 to 4. Do not glue leaves or flower into shell yet. To make tassel, fold decorative cord in half, marking fold with pin. Place fold and one tail of cord at center of shell, arranging cord as shown. Glue in place. Prepare seven silk threads in different colors, each about 20″ (50cm) long. About 2″ (5cm) from edge of shell, twist threads around cord, for about ½″ (1.5cm). Tie securely, letting ends of threads fall freely. Glue leaves in place, then glue flower inside shell.

Decorative thread, such as gold metallic thread or embroidery floss
22″ (55cm) decorative cord (for variation only)
Seven 20″ (50cm) strands of silk thread, each in different color (for variation only)
Craft glue

Variation

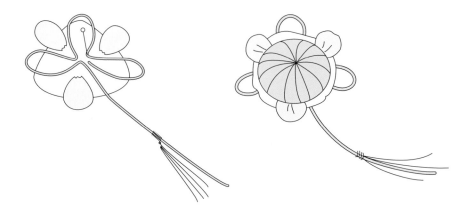

Scents and Secrets

As ancient as the Chinese art of feng shui, the burning of incense has it roots in Buddhist ritual. Incense is thought to calm the mind, heighten the senses, and bring spiritual awareness. In the Heian period (794 to 1194), nobles sought poetic inspiration by "listening to the fragrances." Later, samurai warriors perfumed their helmets with incense to achieve inner peace.

There are more than 500 kinds of incense available in Japan. Some date back to secret formulas created for the Heian court. A very rare example, *jinkoh*, takes decades to form in the root of a special tree. It becomes more precious with the passage of time.

Incense is burned at almost all holiday celebrations. The festival of *O'bon* in mid-August is a unique celebration in which people share the joy of life and the sorrow of death. We visit the graves of our ancestors and burn incense to rouse their spirits.

Some people carry lanterns to guide the spirits back to their homes. For three days, we celebrate *O'bon* with music, folk dancing, and summer games.

Incense is also a natural part of the home. Most families take very special care in creating a *tokomono*, an alcove in which are displayed a seasonal flower arrangement, a hanging scroll, and other items of singular beauty. It is here that incense is burned, filling the home with benevolent scents.

Ko Bukuro

Tucked into the sleeve of a kimono, a Japanese lady carries the fresh scent of lavender wherever she goes. Use the lavender sachet in a closet or lingerie drawer and enjoy its soft aroma.

1. Using Pattern A, cut sachet from patterned fabric. Fold across center as marked.
2. With right sides together, stitch along dotted lines, leaving 2″ (5cm) unstitched on one side and 3½″ (9cm) unstitched on other. Clip curves. Turn right side out and press lightly.
3. Cut three strips measuring 2″ × 4″ (5cm × 10cm) from two complementary fabrics. Set one aside. Fold each of remaining two strips in half lengthwise, right sides out. Fold each in half vertically. Position one folded piece inside the other as shown. Arrange inner piece so that side extends out by approximately ⅛″ (0.4cm) at top, folded edge, reducing to less than ⅛″ (0.4cm) at unfolded, bottom edge. Stitch together along overlap as shown.
4. Insert into 2″ (5cm) opening at top of sachet. Stitch.

Materials

Patterned fabric for outside
of pouch, ⅛ yd (12cm)
Two solid-color or lightly
patterned fabrics, scraps
1 tablespoon lavender
Embroidery floss, cut in eight
lengths of 5″ (13cm) each

Pattern on page 137. Use ¼″ (0.75cm) allowance for all seams.

Step 2

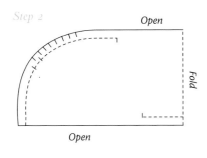

Open

Fold

Open

Step 3

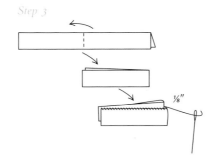

⅛″

Step 4

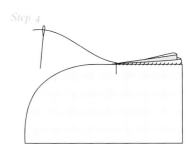

5. Take remaining fabric strip. Fold in half lengthwise, wrong sides out. Stitch ¼″ (0.75cm) from end along dotted line, as shown. Turn right side out.

6. Cut a slightly smaller strip from complementary fabric, measuring 1″ × 3¾″ (2.5cm × 9.5cm). Prepare as in Step 5.

7. Lay smaller piece beneath larger one so that side of larger piece is aligned with dotted line on smaller piece. Make sure points ½″ (1.5cm) from top edge are aligned. Stitch as shown. Stitch pieces in place onto A.

8. Pour one tablespoon lavender into sachet. Insert piece from Step 7 into 3½″ (9cm) opening in A. Arrange a bundle of eight colored threads of embroidery floss, about 5″ (13cm) long. Tie knot in center. Attach threads to edge of A as shown.

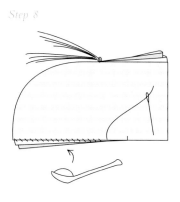

Step 5

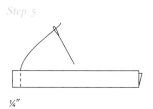

¼″

Step 7

⅜″ ½″

⅛″ ½″

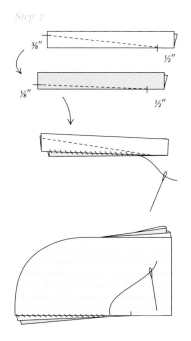

Step 8

Edo Temari

*The sweetly scented chrysanthemum inspired both of the
following designs. The flower is said to keep away evil spirits and
is thought to have medicinal value. Chrysanthemum wine was a
favorite of court nobles in the Edo period (1603 to 1863). Since
ancient times, the flower has been part of the imperial crest, worn
only by the nobility.*

Materials

Two complementary fabrics
for ball, each ⅛ yd (15cm)
or less

Assorted patterned fabrics
for flowers, ⅛ yd (15cm)
or less

Fine embroidery floss

1. Using Pattern A, cut twenty-four; using Pattern B, cut twelve. Right sides together, sew two A pieces to either side of one B piece, joining curved seams. Leave 1″ (2.5cm) opening. Turn right side out and stuff with batting until firm. Blindstitch opening closed to complete cone shape.

2. Join two cones into a pair at tips with one or two stitches. In same way, join a second pair. Connect two pairs to make a four-cone unit.

3. Join two cones into a pair at point A with one or two stitches. In same way, join a second pair. Connect two pairs to make a four-cone unit. Repeat.

4. Cut eight strips measuring 1¾″ × 6¼″ (4.6cm × 16cm). Join side seams to make loop. Mark side and center points as shown. Pull four points to center to make four small loops. Baste in place. Stitch top seams of each loop. Remove basting. Knot four strands of embroidery floss together, with knot about ½″ (1.5cm) from tail. One at a time, draw each strand through center point, from right side to the wrong side. Leave a tail of about 2″ (5cm) on the wrong side. Turn right side out. Gather-stitch bottom, drawing loose tails of embroidery floss through to tip of flower. Pull stitches tight and backstitch to hold. Make eight flowers.

5. Attach loose tail of each flower to center of four-cone unit you made in Step 2, allowing flower to dangle about 2″ (5cm) from center.

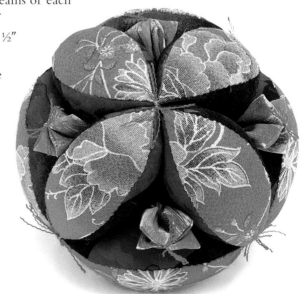

6. To construct ball, attach units from Step 3 to either side of unit from Step 5, securing with one or two stitches where tops of cones meet.

7. Pull flowers gently from center so that a blossom nestles in each of the hollows in ball. If desired, make a tiny fringe at each of the six points on ball where cone tips meet. Double-fold a 2″ (5cm) strand of embroidery thread and stitch to tip. Snip loops.

Variation

A simpler version of *Edo Temari* can be made by omitting the flowers in Steps 4 and 7. Instead, make two decorative fringes to attach to either side. To make fringe, fold twenty 3½″ (9cm) strands of fine embroidery floss in half. Wrap and tie with floss about ½″ (1.5cm) from fold to hold. Position and stitch fringe at opposite sides of ball.

Patterns on page 138. Use ¼″ (0.75cm) allowance for all seams.

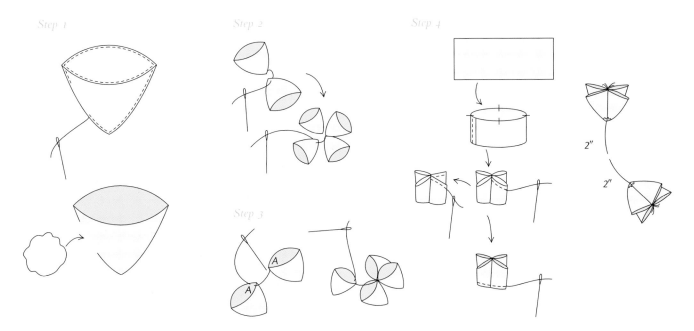

Step 1

Step 2

Step 3

Step 4

2″

2″

Kusadama

This beautiful flowered scent bag might release its delicate perfume at a formal tea ceremony, where guests will admire its intricate design and breathe in its refreshing aromas. A Japanese lady might use it to hold her tea utensils.

1. Using Patterns A and B, cut one bottom hexagon and twelve side pentagons from plain white cotton. Using rotary cutter and mat or scissors, cut fabric squares from assorted patterned fabrics in the following sizes.

Base square C	1½″ × 1½″	(4cm × 4cm)	Cut 3
Base square D	2″ × 2″	(5.4cm × 5.4cm)	Cut 3
Base square E	2½″ × 2½″	(6.5cm × 6.5cm)	Cut 6
Side square F	1½″ × 1½″	(4cm × 4cm)	Cut 36
Side square G	1¾″ × 1¾″	(4.6cm × 4.6cm)	Cut 36
Side square H	2″ × 2″	(5.4cm × 5.4cm)	Cut 60

2. Place thin layer of cotton from cotton ball onto wrong side of each square C to H. Fold in half diagonally to create triangles, then baste.

3. Position three F triangles on side pentagon B, matching center points of long sides of triangles and overlapping. Pin in place, then stitch.

Materials

Plain white cotton, ¼ yd (25cm) or less

Assorted patterned fabrics, ¼ yd (25cm) or less

Fabric for lining, ¼ yd (25cm) or less

Cotton/polyester batting

Two 26″ (66cm) ribbons or drawstrings

Lavender or incense

Patterns on page 138. Use ¼″ (0.75cm) allowance for all seams.

Step 2

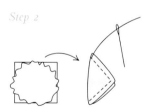

Step 3

Step 4

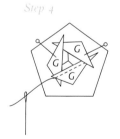

Step 5

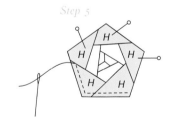

4. Position three G triangles on side pentagon B, covering edges of F triangles and overlapping as shown.

5. Position five H triangles on side pentagon B, covering edges of G triangles and overlapping as shown.

6. Repeat Steps 3 to 5 to complete a total of twelve side pieces.

7. Position three C triangles, three D triangles, and six E triangles on bottom hexagon A, using same method described in Steps 3 to 5.

8. Right sides together, stitch one side of each completed side pentagon to completed bottom hexagon. Stitch side seams, joining pentagons. Add remaining six pentagons to first six in same way. Turn right side out.

9. Cut a strip of fabric for lining, measuring 6½″ × 16″ (16.5cm × 40.6cm). Right sides together, fold in half lengthwise and stitch seam. Baste along bottom edge and pull thread tight to gather. Backstitch to hold. Wrong sides together, position lining inside bag. Stitch in place around top edge.

10. Cut two strips measuring 4″ × 7″ (10.6cm × 18cm) for hems. Follow directions for making hems on page xvii.

11. To create fabric beads, cut two squares measuring 2″ × 2″ (5.4cm × 5.4cm). Follow directions for Method 1 on page xvii.

12. Fill bag with lavender or incense. Tie as desired.

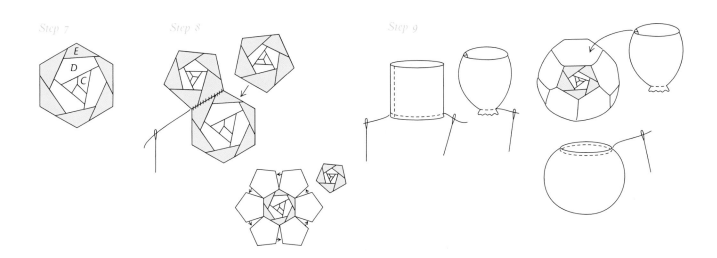

Step 7 *Step 8* *Step 9*

Pandora

Pandora makes a pretty hiding place for secret notes or love tokens. In Greek legend, Zeus gave Pandora a box containing all human ills, which escaped when she opened the box. Hope, alone, remained.

1. Using Pattern A, cut four from cardboard (no seam allowance); cut two from fabric for outside lid and outside bottom, and two more from lining fabric for inside lid and inside bottom (add seam allowance). Gather-stitch around seam allowances, wrapping cardboard, and pull stitches tight. Backstitch to hold.

2. For lid, cut strip of cardboard measuring 1″ × 10½″ (2.5cm × 26.6cm); cut slightly wider strip from fabric, measuring 1⅛″ × 10½″ (2.9cm × 26.6cm). Score cardboard from end to end ¼″ (0.75cm) from top for easy folding. Make ¼″ (0.75cm) clips all along top edge. Glue or tape ends, overlapping by ½″ (1.5cm) to make loop. Cover outside with fabric, starting ⅛″ (0.4cm) from top, above clipped edge. Wrap extra fabric to inside, covering bottom edge. Push clipped edge gently to inside.

3. Spread glue about ¼″ (0.75cm) around outer edge of wrong side of card circle wrapped in lining fabric. Position beneath loop and push up, attaching lid lining to turned-in clipped edge of loop. Press firmly until dry. Cut strip measuring ¾″ × 10½″ (2cm × 26.6cm) from lining fabric. Glue to inside of loop.

4. For base, cut strip of cardboard measuring 1¼″ × 10½″ (3.2cm × 26.6cm); cut one slightly wider from fabric measuring 1⅝″ × 10½″ (4.4cm × 26.6cm). Score card strip lengthwise with craft knife, ¼″ (0.75cm) from bottom edge. Make ¼″ (0.75cm) clips all along bottom edge for easy folding. Glue or tape ends, overlapping by ½″ (1.5cm) to make loop. Cover outside with fabric, starting ⅛″

Materials

Large sheet of cardboard

Patterned fabrics for outer box, bottom, and lid, ¼ yd (25cm) or less

Fabric for lining, ⅛ yd (15cm) or less

Craft glue

Embroidery floss or metallic thread

Pattern on page 139. Use ¼″ (0.75cm) allowance for all seams.

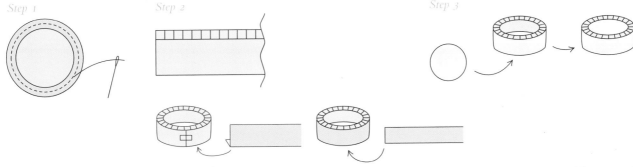

Step 1   Step 2   Step 3

(0.4cm) from bottom, ⅛″ (0.4cm) below clipped edge. Wrap extra fabric to inside, covering top edge. Push clipped edge gently to inside.

5. For inside rim, cut strip of cardboard measuring 1¼″ × 10½″ (3.2cm × 26.6cm). Glue ends, overlapping by ½″ (1.5cm), to make loop. Cut strip of lining fabric measuring 1½″ × 10½″ (4cm × 26.6cm). Glue to inside of loop, starting at top and wrapping about ¼″ (0.75cm) around to outside. Insert completed rim inside base. Taking circle covered with lining fabric from Step 1, glue about ½″ (1.5cm) around outer edge of wrong side. Position above loop and push down, attaching lined bottom to base. Press firmly until dry. Glue circle wrapped in patterned fabric in place for bottom of box.

6. Decorate outside lid from Step 1 with embroidery floss or metallic thread. Begin by placing ten pins at points 1 to 10 shown. Tape end of thread inside lid. Bring to front and draw across lid from 1 to 4. Wrap around back of lid, emerging again at point 7 and drawing across to point 10. Repeat, this time beginning at point 3 (point 3 over to point 6; under to point 9; over to point 2). Repeat again, beginning at point 5 (point 5 over to point 8; under to point 1). Repeat this three-step process four more times, leaving space of ⅛″ (0.4cm) or less between each strand of thread. Tape end of thread to back of lid. Glue completed lid in place onto box top.

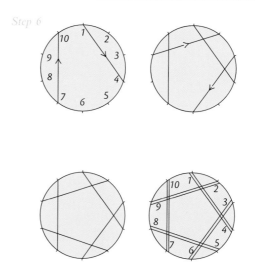

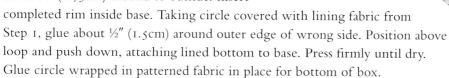

Step 5

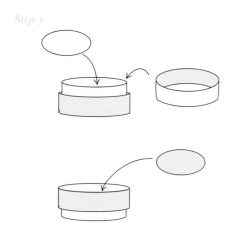

Step 6

Fortune Catcher

Hang Fortune Catcher *in a doorway or from a fan pull to ward off mischief and make your wishes come true.*

1. Using Pattern A, cut two from cardboard (no seam allowance); cut one from fabric (add seam allowance). Using Pattern B, cut one from fabric (add seam allowance). Gather-stitch fabric A around seam allowances, wrapping one of cardboard circles, and pull stitches tight. Backstitch to hold.

2. Place a little batting on surface of second cardboard circle. Gather-stitch fabric B around seam allowance, wrapping circle and batting inside, and pull stitches tight. Backstitch to hold.

3. Cut 4″ (10cm) off 30″ (76cm) strand of decorative string. Fold 4″ (10cm) length in half. At about ¾″ (2cm) below fold, tie center point of remaining 26″ (66cm) length of string. Make two square knots, following directions on page xix. Pull about 1″ (2.5cm) of string out to each side to make loops of bow. Make two more square knots. Leave a 5″ (13cm) tail at end of each string, snipping rest away. Make knot at each end.

4. Glue or stitch ends of 4″ (10cm) string to back of padded circle so that knots and bow rest at tip of ornament.

5. To make fringe, fold twenty 3½″ (9cm) strands of fine embroidery floss in half and tie at center. Alternatively, buy completed fringe from craft store. Position and stitch fringe at center bottom of padded circle. Wrong sides together, blindstitch two covered circles together.

Materials

Sheet of cardboard
Patterned fabrics for front
 and back, ⅛ yd (15cm)
 or less
Craft knife
Craft glue
30″ (76cm) decorative string
Fine embroidery floss or
 finished fringe

Patterns on page 139. Use ¼″ (0.75cm) allowance for all seams.

Step 1

Step 2

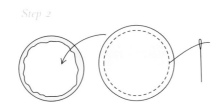

Step 3

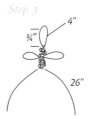

¾″ 4″

26″

Step 4

Step 5

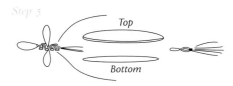

Top

Bottom

Ohgi

Light, delicate, and oh, so secretive, fans were used by the ladies of the imperial court in Kyoto to hide amorous glances and carry on sweet flirtations. A highly valued gift, fans are a charming accessory on formal and informal occasions.

1. Using Pattern A, cut two from cardboard for lid (no seam allowance); cut one from fabric for outside lid and one from lining fabric for inside lid (add seam allowance). Clip seam allowance along bottom curve. Tape sides and bottom curve to cardboard, turning in seam allowance. Gather-stitch top curve, wrapping cardboard, and pull stitches tight. Backstitch to hold. Repeat with Pattern B to prepare pieces for outside bottom and inside bottom.

2. To prepare lid, cut strip of cardboard measuring 1¼″ × 11½″ (3.2cm × 29cm); cut one from fabric, measuring 1½″ × 11½″ (4cm × 29.3cm). Cut one slightly smaller from lining fabric, measuring ⅞″ × 11¼″ (2.2cm × 28cm). Mark and score vertical lines on cardboard as shown. Mark and score lengthwise, ¼″ (0.75cm) from top edge. Make ¼″ (0.75cm) clips along sections 2 and 4 of top edge for easy folding. Glue fabric to outside, aligning along clipped edge and wrapping around edge of lid. Glue lining to inside. Trim if necessary.

3. Fold vertical score lines to make fan shape. Glue ends, overlapping by ½″ (1.5cm). Push clipped edges gently to inside.

Materials

Sheet of cardboard

Patterned fabrics for outer box, bottom, and lid, ¼ yd (25cm) or less

Fabric for lining, ⅛ yd (15cm) or less

Scraps for fabric beads

Cotton/polyester batting

Craft glue

Fine embroidery floss or metallic thread

50″ (127cm) decorative string or thick embroidery floss

Patterns on page 140. Use ¼″ (0.75cm) allowance for all seams.

Patterns on page 140.

Step 1

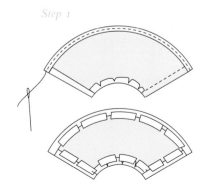

Step 2

½″
(1.5cm)

1¾″ (4.4cm)	1¾″ (4.4cm)	1¾″ (4.4cm)	5¾″ (14.6cm)	1¼″ (3.2cm)
1	2	3	4	

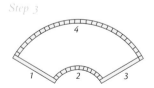

Step 3

4
1	2	3

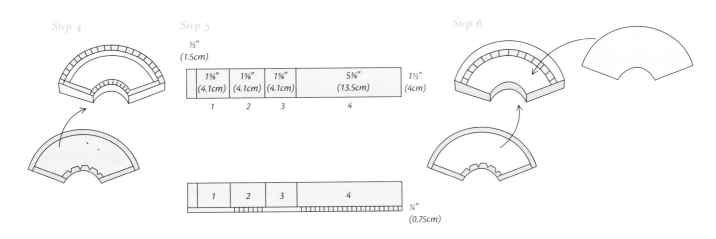

4. Spread glue about ¼" (0.75cm) around outer edge of wrong side of Pattern A cardboard wrapped in lining fabric. Position beneath fan shape and push up, attaching lid lining to clipped edge of fan shape. Press firmly until dry.

5. To prepare bottom, cut strip of cardboard measuring 1½" × 10¾" (4cm × 27.3cm); cut one from fabric, measuring 1¾" × 10¾" (4.4cm × 27.3cm). Cut one slightly smaller from lining fabric, measuring 1¼" × 10¾" (3.2cm × 27.3cm). Mark and score vertical lines on cardboard as shown. Mark and score lengthwise, ¼" (0.75cm) from bottom edge. Make ¼" (0.75cm) clips along bottom edge of sections 2 and 4 for easy folding. Glue fabric to outside, aligning along clipped edge, wrapping around edge of lid. Glue lining to inside. Trim if necessary.

6. Fold vertical score lines to make fan shape. Glue ends, overlapping by ½" (1.5cm). Push clipped edges gently to inside. Spread glue about ¼" (0.75cm) around outer edge of wrong side of Pattern B cardboard wrapped in lining fabric. Position above fan shape and push down, attaching bottom lining to turned-in clipped edge of fan shape. Press firmly until dry. Glue Pattern B cardboard wrapped in outer fabric to bottom of fan shape.

7. Decorate covered lid from Step 1 with embroidery floss or metallic thread. Begin by placing twenty-two pins at equal distances around entire outer curve.

Step 4

Step 5

½"
(1.5cm)

1⅝" (4.1cm)	1⅝" (4.1cm)	1⅝" (4.1cm)	5⅜" (13.5cm)	1½" (4cm)
1	2	3	4	

1	2	3	4	

¼"
(0.75cm)

Step 6

Place another twenty-two pins along entire inner curve. Tape end of thread inside lid. Bring to front and draw across lid from first pin on outer curve to first pin on inner curve. Wrap around back, emerging again at second pin on outer curve. Wrap back and forth until thread is drawn evenly across entire fan shape. Tape end of thread to back.

8. Cut five 10″ (25cm) strands of decorative string or heavy embroidery floss. Tape ends of two strands in position at inner curve on underside of lid. Tie strands about ½″ (1.5cm) from lid. Following directions on page xix, make two square knots. Pull about ¾″ (2cm) of string out to each side to make loops of bow. Make two more square knots.

9. To make fabric beads, cut three using Pattern C. Gather-stitch around seam allowance, stuffing with batting, and pull thread tight. Knot one end of each of three remaining strands of decorative string. Stuff into beads. Backstitch to hold. Gather three strands about ½″ (1.5cm) away from beads, wrapping and tying one around other two to hold securely in place. Make four more square knots. Thread ends through bottom knot made in Step 8. Tie off ends of all five strands neatly and snip away loose ends.

10. Glue completed lid in place onto box top.

Step 7

Step 9

Fragrance

A dancer in Kabuki *theater deftly waves a fan to mask his emotions and entrance his audience. Fill Fragrance with sweet jasmine or lavender, and let its sweet perfume calm your spirits.*

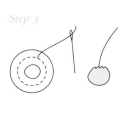

1. Using Pattern A, cut two from cardboard (no seam allowance); cut two from decorative paper, such as *origami* paper or gift wrap (no seam allowance); cut two from fabric (add seam allowance). Clip seam allowance along bottom curve. Tape sides and bottom curve to cardboard, turning in seam allowance. Gather-stitch top curve, wrapping cardboard, and pull stitches tight, Backstitch to hold. Glue paper to wrong side, trimming edges neatly.

2. Beginning about 10″ (25cm) from one end, attach one edge of ribbon with overcast stitch to first fan shape, progressing from point 1 to 2, point 2 to 3, and point 3 to 4. In same way, attach other edge of ribbon to second fan shape.

3. To make fabric beads (if desired), cut three using Pattern B. Gather-stitch around seam allowance, stuffing with batting. Knot one end of each of three 1½″ (4cm) strands of embroidery floss. Stuff into beads and pull gathering stitches tight. Backstitch to hold. Glue loose end of each strand to inside of fan shape, allowing beads to fall onto fan.

4. Insert four tablespoons of lavender, jasmine, or other fragrance through opening. Loosely tie ribbon.

Materials

Sheet of cardboard

Patterned fabrics, ⅛ yd (15cm) or less

Sheet of *origami* paper or gift wrap

Scraps for fabric beads

Craft knife

Craft glue

36″ (90cm) ribbon

Embroidery floss

4 tablespoons lavender, jasmine, or other fragrance

Patterns on page 140. Use ¼″ (0.75cm) allowance for all seams.

Step 1

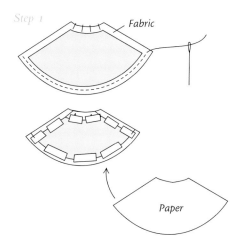

Fabric

Paper

Step 2

Step 3

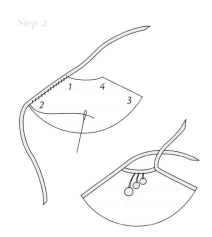

Whimsy

When I was eight years old, I moved from the bustling city of Tokyo to the suburbs of Kamakura to live with my aunt. This was the beginning of a new life, a life filled with the sights and sounds of nature in the quiet, forested mountains of Kamakura. Each day, as I walked home from school through ancient woodland that was the site of a thousand-year-old Shinto shrine, I absorbed the wonders of nature. I loved the plants, the flowers, the fallen leaves, and, most of all, the delightful woodland creatures who brightened my days with their playful antics.

It was my aunt who taught me to sew. She would give me scraps of wonderful, lustrous silks from her wooden sewing box. I would twist them and turn them, enjoying their colors and textures, much as another child might play with *origami* papers.

Now, as I relax in my backyard in the hills of Oregon, my thoughts turn again to the bright days of my childhood. As I stitch, those tiny woodland creatures I remember so well come to life in fabric in my hands. When I give them as gifts, I share my most cherished memories.

Butterfly

A popular motif in the Nara period (710 to 794), the butterfly protected against evil spirits. Later, during the Kamakura era (1185 to 1333), the butterfly danced on helmets and suits of armor, a symbol of rebirth, prosperity, and good fortune. The tiny pocket in Butterfly *can hold a good luck charm.*

Materials

Assorted patterned fabrics
   for body and wings,
   ⅛ (15cm) or less
Solid fabric for wing backs,
   ⅛ yd (15cm) or less
Fabric for pocket, scraps
Two 12″ (30cm) drawstrings
   or ribbons
Two 8″ (20cm) strands of
   embroidery floss for
   antennae

1. Using Pattern A, cut two body pieces. Right sides together, stitch as shown, leaving top open. Clip curves. Turn right side out.
2. Using Pattern B, cut four wing pieces, reversing the pattern for two. Choose patterned fabric for front of wings and plain for backs. Match pairs. Right sides together, stitch as shown, leaving side open. Clip curves. Turn right side out.
3. Choose shape of under-wing, Pattern C1 or C2. Cut four under-wing pieces, reversing the pattern for two. Choose patterned fabric for fronts and plain for backs. Match pairs. Right sides together, stitch as shown, leaving side open. Clip curves. Turn right side out.

Patterns on page 141. Use ¼″ (0.75cm) allowance for all seams.

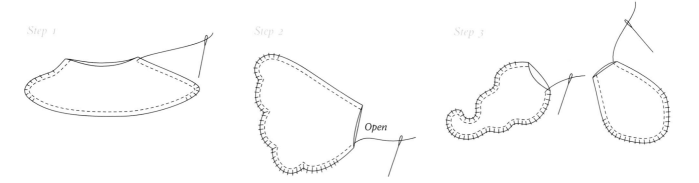

Step 1   Step 2   Open   Step 3

4. Pin wings and under-wings in place around opening in body. Stitch raw edges together to open raw edge of body.

5. Using Pattern D, cut two pocket pieces. Right sides together, stitch curved seam, leaving top open.

6. Cut two hem pieces measuring 1½″ × 3″ (4cm × 7.8cm). Follow directions on making hems on page xvi.

7. Using a large needle or knitting needle, thread string through head, about ¼″ (0.75cm) in from tip. Knot string as close as possible to either side of head. Make two more knots 3″ (7.6cm) away from first two. Fray ends of string.

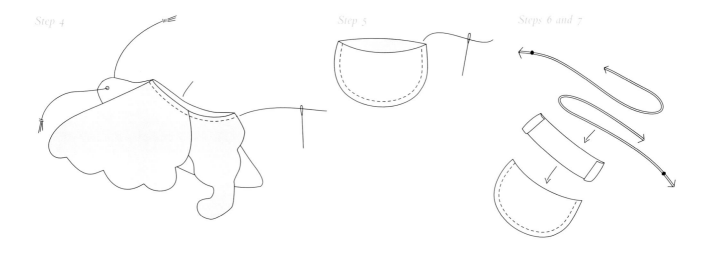

Step 4

Step 5

Steps 6 and 7

Pine Cone

松笠

This Pine Cone pouch makes a wonderful gift for New Year, one of the most popular holidays in Japan. We use pine to decorate our family shrines, street corners, and gateways. A gift at New Year is a wish for prosperity in the future.

1. Using Pattern A, cut seven. Cut twenty-eight B squares from light fabric measuring 1¾″ × 1¾″ (4.6cm × 4.6cm). Repeat with second, darker fabric. Cut seven C strips measuring 1¾″ × 2⅞″ (4.6cm × 7.6cm).

2. Pair one light square with one dark square. Right sides together, sew two seams as shown, beginning and ending ¼″ (0.75cm) from edges. Press. Turn right side out. Make twenty-eight.

3. Position one light/dark pair on work surface so that sewn corner is at right front and light fabric faces up. Place second pair on top of first, with sewn corner at left front and light fabric facing up. Pin bottom layer of top pair (dark) to top layer of bottom pair (light). Stitch seam. Take care not to sew into ¼″ (0.75cm) seam allowance. Add third and fourth pairs to this unit in same way.

4. Right sides together, stitch piece A to raw edge at right of dark fabric in first pair. Stitch piece C to raw edge at left of light fabric in fourth pair.

Materials

Patterned fabrics for outer bag, hem, and beads, ¼ yd (25cm) or less

Fabric for lining, ¼ yd (25cm) or less

Two 28″ (70cm) ribbons or drawstrings

Pattern on page 142. Use ¼″ (0.75cm) allowance for all seams.

Step 2

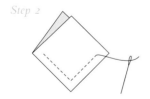

Step 3

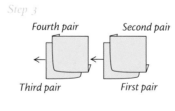

Fourth pair   Second pair

Third pair   First pair

Step 4

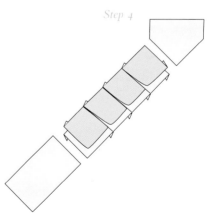

5. Repeat Steps 3 and 4 to make seven sets.

6. Place seven sets side by side. Join as shown. Join ends, stitching first set to last set to form a tube with seven "triangles" of fabric at bottom.

7. Fold in triangles, pin together, and stitch seams to form outer pouch. Turn right side out.

8. Cut a 4½″ × 10″ (11.5cm × 25cm) strip for lining. Right sides together, stitch short edges to form tube. Gather-stitch along bottom seam allowance. Pull stitches tight to gather. Backstitch to hold. Place lining inside bag. Pin and baste in place along top edges.

9. Cut two strips measuring 1½″ × 6½″ (4cm × 16.5cm) for hems. Follow directions on making hems on page xvi.

10. To create fabric beads, cut two squares of fabric measuring 2″ × 2″ (5cm × 5cm). Follow directions for Method 1 on page xvii.

Step 6

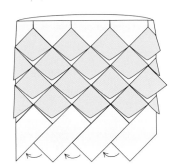

Step 7

Step 8

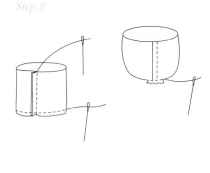

Sparrow

In my backyard in the rolling hills of Oregon, the birds keep me company as I sew, stealing colorful threads to make their nests high in the treetops. This little sparrow makes a pretty purse—let him take care of your loose change.

1. Using Pattern A, cut one from patterned fabric for head. Using Pattern B, cut two from patterned fabric and two from lining for body. Transfer markings. Using Pattern C, cut two from patterned fabric (reverse for one) and two from lining for wings (reverse for one). Using Pattern D, cut one from patterned fabric and one from lining for tail.

2. Right sides together, stitch wing to wing lining, leaving side seam open. Turn right side out. Repeat for second wing. In same way, stitch tail to tail lining, leaving top open. Turn right side out.

3. Pin wings and tail in place onto right side of top body piece. Place bottom body on top, right side down. Stitch around seam allowances, trapping wings and tail, and leaving top open. Turn right side out.

Materials

Assorted patterned fabrics for body, head, wings, tail, and beak, ⅛ yd (15cm) or less

Lining fabric for underside of wings and tail and inner pocket, ⅛ yd (15cm) or less

Fine-tip marker, black

Cotton/polyester batting

Two 20" (50cm) ribbons or drawstrings

Patterns on page 142. Use ¼" (0.75cm) allowance for all seams.

Step 2

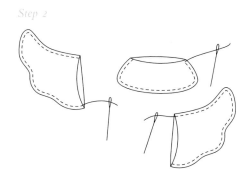

Step 3

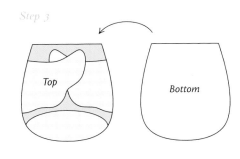

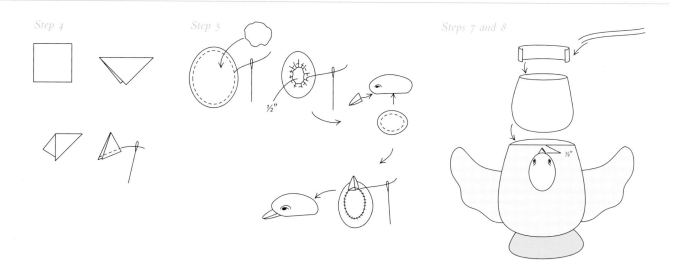

4. Cut 1″ × 1″ (2.5cm × 2.5cm) square for beak. Fold across diagonal three times to make small triangle. Baste bottom edge.

5. Gather-stitch seam allowance of head A, stuffing with batting. Pull stitches until opening is about ½″ (1.5cm). Backstitch to hold. Using Pattern E, cut small oval. Turn under seam allowance and baste in place. Pin beak at bottom edge of head. Stitch piece E to bottom of head, trapping beak in place.

6. Sew head to body, ½″ (1.5cm) below opening. Draw eyes with fine-tip marker.

7. Right sides together, stitch seam allowances on body lining B, leaving top open. Insert lining into opening in body. Pin and then baste raw edges together.

8. Cut two strips measuring 1½″ × 3½″ (4cm × 9cm) for hems. Follow directions on making hems on page xvi. Tie ribbons or drawstrings as desired.

Step 4

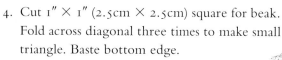

Step 5

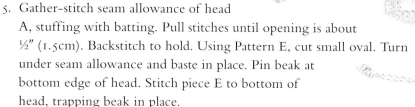

Steps 7 and 8

Tsuru

A popular image in Japanese origami, the crane symbolizes freedom. Give Tsuru as a good luck charm for a new baby, or to top a gift.

1. On fabric square, mark center point of each side and points A to D, as shown.
2. Wrong side out, fold diagonally, matching points A. Stitch 2½" (6.4cm) from center point to diagonal.
3. Repeat, matching points B, then points D. Match points C and stitch, leaving 1" (2.5cm) open at center. Turn right side out.
4. Stuff with lavender. You can vary the shape of the crane by varying the amount of lavender. Blindstitch opening closed.
5. Position as shown with Point C nearest you. Point C forms head; points A and D form wings; point B forms tail. To create head, fold tip of point C by about 1" (2.5cm) as shown. Stitch once or twice to hold to main body at left and right of fold line.
6. To create wings, fold tips of points A and D in by about 1¾" (4.4cm) as shown. Stitch once or twice at point shown to hold.
7. Form tail by tugging point B and molding to a point with hands. Continue to mold shape of bird as desired with hands.

Materials

Square of patterned fabric,
 5½" × 5½"
 (14.5cm × 14.5cm)
4 tablespoons lavender

Use ¼" (0.75cm) allowance for all seams.

Step 1

A   C

A   C

B   D

B   D

Step 2

A

A   2½"

Step 3

A

B   2½"

B   A

D   C

Step 4

B   D

A   C

1"

Step 5

B

A   D

1"   C

Step 6

D

1¾"

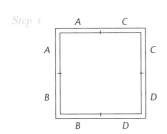
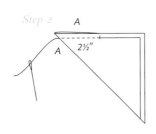
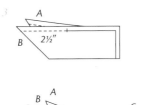
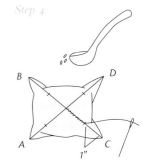
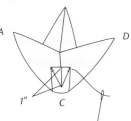

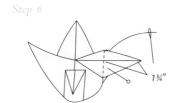

Squirrel

Untie the knot, and this fanciful woodland creature turns into a handy pouch. Keep him on your shelf to hold glittering jewelry or shiny coins.

1. Using Patterns A to C, cut two each for body, head, and tail. Clip lines in body A and head B. Transfer marking on B for placement of eye. Using Pattern D, cut eight for paws. Using Pattern E, cut two eyes from felt (no seam allowance needed). Cut two ½″ × ½″ (1.5cm × 1.5cm) felt squares for ears.
2. Fold ears as shown. Slide into clipped line in head and stitch in place. Stitch eyes to head.
3. Right sides together, stitch around seam allowances, leaving neck open. Turn right side out. Embroider a few stitches at nose. Right sides together, sew paws and tail, leaving short edges open. Turn right side out. Use toothpick to smooth curves.
4. Right sides together, pin body front to back, matching clip lines. Slide head, tail, and paws in position between fabrics as shown. Pin again. Sew curved seam, trapping pieces in place. Leave top open. Turn right side out.

Materials

Patterned fabrics for body, head, and paws, ⅛ yd (15cm) or less

Complementary fabric for cover and lid, scraps

Felt scraps for eyes and ears

Fabric for pocket lining and lid lining, ⅛ yd (15cm) or less

Embroidery floss

Cotton/polyester batting

Two 10″ (25cm) drawstrings

Patterns on pages 143–144. Use ¼″ (0.75cm) allowance for all seams.

Step 2

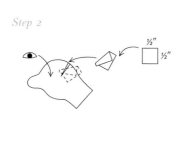

Step 3

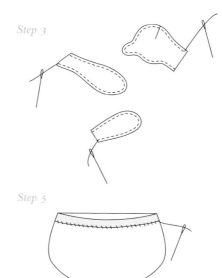

Step 4

Step 5

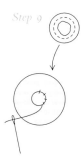

5. Using Pattern F, cut two from lining fabric. Transfer all markings. Baste darts. Right sides together, stitch curved seam. Fold top edge to wrong side by ¼″ (0.75cm). Repeat. Press in place. Insert lining into body. Slip-stitch in place.

6. Using Pattern G, cut two from fabric and two from lining for cover. Sew side seams. Turn right side out and open out. Turn under and press top and bottom seam allowances. Repeat with lining. Pin and then slip-stitch folded edge of lining to top of cover, trapping ends of drawstrings between cover and lining.

7. Place completed cover on top of body. Slip-stitch in place around bottom edge.

8. Using Pattern H, cut two from cardboard (no seam allowance); cut one from fabric and one from lining (add seam allowance). Gather-stitch each around seam allowances, trapping circle of cardboard inside. Wrong sides together, slip-stitch lid top to lid lining around edges.

9. Using Pattern I, cut one knob. Gather-stitch around seam allowance, stuffing with batting. Pull stitches tight. Backstitch to hold. Stitch to center of lid. Attach completed lid with two or three stitches to top edge of cover, above tail. Pull drawstrings to top of lid and tie as desired.

Step 6

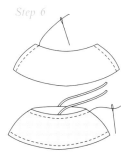

Step 7

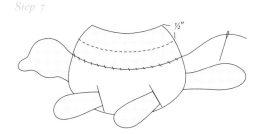

½″

Step 8

Step 9

Goldfish

Long ago, goldfish were popular as pets with the aristocracy of the imperial court in Kyoto. Today, there are hundreds of varieties, and goldfish peddlers are often seen at temples and shrines during festival times. Children will love this fishy-purse as a gift.

1. Using Pattern A, cut two from patterned fabric for body and two from plain fabric for lining. Transfer markings to body pieces.

2. Using Pattern B, cut four fins, reversing pattern for two. Right sides together, stitch first two fins, leaving top open. Turn right side out. Fold under seam allowance along opening and press. Repeat for second fin. Stitch fins in position onto body along open edge only. Cut scraps of black and white felt for eyes and stitch in place. Right sides together, stitch side seams. Turn right side out.

3. Using Pattern C, cut two tail pieces. Right sides together, stitch all but straight seam at left. Clip angles and curves. Turn right side out.

4. Using Pattern D, cut one bag base from patterned fabric and one from plain fabric for lining. Pin tail in position to right side of base. Right sides together, stitch base to body bottom, securing tail. Turn right side out.

5. To make pocket, place body lining pieces right sides together and stitch side seams. Right sides together, stitch base lining around bottom of body lining. Wrong sides together, position lining inside bag. Stitch in place around top edge.

6. Cut two strips measuring 1½″ × 5″ (4cm × 12.8cm). Follow directions on page xvi for making hems.

Materials

Assorted patterned fabrics for body, fins, tail, and base, ⅛ yd (15cm) or less

Fabric for bag lining, ⅛ yd (15cm) or less

Black and white felt scraps for eyes

Two 15″ (38cm) drawstrings or ribbons

Patterns on pages 144-145. Use ¼″ (0.75cm) allowance for all seams.

Step 2   Step 3   Step 4   Step 5

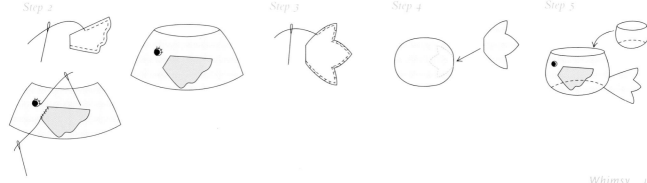

Cicada

Higurashi, *the cicada, is a symbol of new life through reincarnation. Emerging from the larva stage only once every seventeen years, thousands of cicadas, their shells an unusual mix of blue and green, cover the summer fields. Their sad, lonely song has moved the hearts of poets.*

1. Using Patterns A, B, and C, cut tail pieces. Do not add seam allowances to B and C. Fold B and C in half lengthwise. Lay folded B on top of A, aligning raw edges as shown, and stitch. Repeat, folding and stitching three tail pieces C.

2. Using Pattern D, cut front body piece. Right sides together, stitch body to tail.

3. Using Pattern E, cut back body piece. Right sides together, stitch front body to back body, leaving 1¼" (3.2cm) open at top of each side seam. Clip curves. Turn right side out.

4. Again using Pattern E, cut two for inner pouch. Right sides together, stitch along sides and bottom. Use ⅜" (1cm) seam allowance so that inner pouch is slightly smaller than body. Position inside outer body and pin in place.

Materials

Assortment of patterned
  fabrics, ¼ yd (25cm) or less
Fabric for inner pouch
Cotton/polyester batting
Two 15" (38cm) drawstrings
  or ribbons

Patterns on pages 145-148. Use ¼" (0.75cm) allowance for all seams.

Step 1

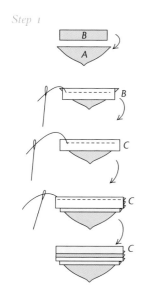

Step 2

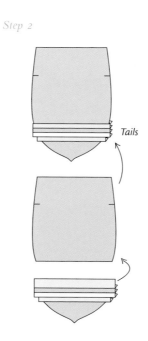

Tails

Step 3

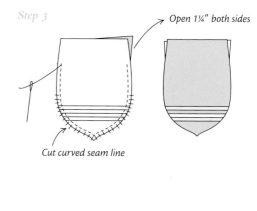

Open 1¼" both sides

Cut curved seam line

5. Using Pattern F, cut eight wing pieces, reversing pattern for four. Place two right sides together and stitch as shown, leaving top open. Clip curves and turn right side out. Repeat to complete all four wings.

6. With body front facing, position first wing at slight angle to side of body and at a distance of about ¼" (0.75cm) from top center, as shown. Position second wing on other side. Pin in place. Arrange remaining wings on top of first two, so that about ½" (1.5cm) of lower wing shows. Pin. Stitch all wings in place onto body front and front of inner pouch.

Step 5

Step 6

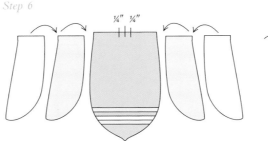

¼" ¼"

7. Using Patterns G, H, and I, cut two of each head piece. Right sides together, sew pairs to create three head sections. Clip curves and turn right side out. Position with largest piece on bottom and smallest on top. Pin in place. Position as shown on body front and stitch in place.

8. Using Pattern J, cut two eyes. Do not add seam allowance. Place stuffing at center, wrapping fabric over it. Tighten and secure with a few stitches, as shown. Sew eyes to top edge of head, about 1″ (2.5cm) apart and ¼″ (0.75cm) from top.

9. Cut two strips measuring 2″ × 5″ (5cm × 12.8cm) for hems. Follow directions for making hems on page xvi.

10. To create fabric beads, cut out two circles of fabric using Pattern K. Do not add seam allowance. Gather-stitch around circle. Stuff and pull thread gently to gather. Stuff knotted ends of ribbons or drawstrings inside fabric bead. Pull gathering stitches tight. Double-stitch to hold.

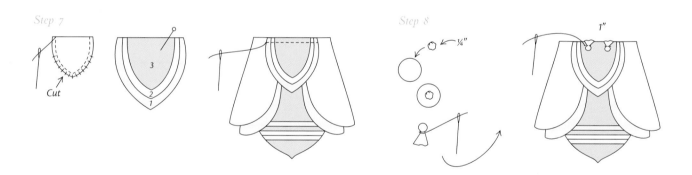

Step 7

Cut

3

2
1

Step 8

¼″

1″

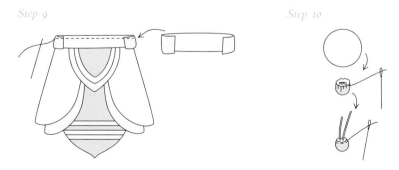

Step 9

Step 10

Bunny

Easy to make in colorful fabrics, this little bunny makes an ideal gift for a child at Easter time.

1. Using Pattern A, cut two from patterned fabric for body and two from plain fabric for pocket lining. Transfer all markings. Using Pattern B, cut two paws. Appliqué a paw to each body piece. Using Pattern C, cut two eye pieces from felt. Do not add seam allowance. Stitch to body.
2. Right sides together, stitch around body, leaving about 2″ (5cm) open at center top and about ¾″ (2cm) open at tail, as marked. Clip curves. Turn right side out.
3. Using Pattern D, cut two tail pieces. Right sides together, stitch around curve. Clip curves. Turn right side out. Stuff with batting. Blindstitch opening closed. Insert tail into opening on body. Blindstitch closed.
4. Open out body and stuff base lightly with batting. To make pouch, place body lining pieces right sides together and stitch side seams. Gather-stitch along bottom and pull stitches tight. Backstitch to hold. Wrong sides together, position pouch inside bunny. Fold in raw edges of body top and top pocket. Pin and stitch to complete opening of pouch.
5. Using Pattern E, cut four ear pieces. Choose patterned fabric for fronts and solids for backs. Match pairs. Right sides together, stitch all but marked opening. Turn right side out. Blindstitch opening closed. Pinch top of ear to make slight tuck. Stitch in place over tuck.
6. With embroidery floss, make a single stitch to mark mouth. Make two neat stitches at tip of each paw. Hide ends of threads inside body.

Materials

Assorted patterned fabrics for body, ears, tail, and paws, ⅛ yd (15cm) or less

Solid fabric for backs of ears, scraps

Felt scraps for eyes

Fabric for pocket lining, ⅛ yd (15cm) or less

Embroidery floss

Cotton/polyester batting

Patterns on page 149. Use ¼″ (0.75cm) allowance for all seams.

Step 1

Step 3

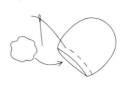

Step 5

Patterns

Panache!

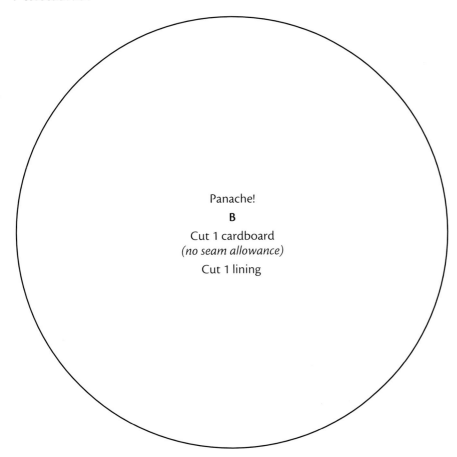

Panache!

B

Cut 1 cardboard
(no seam allowance)

Cut 1 lining

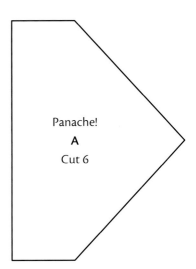

Panache!
A
Cut 6

Sea Bream Dream

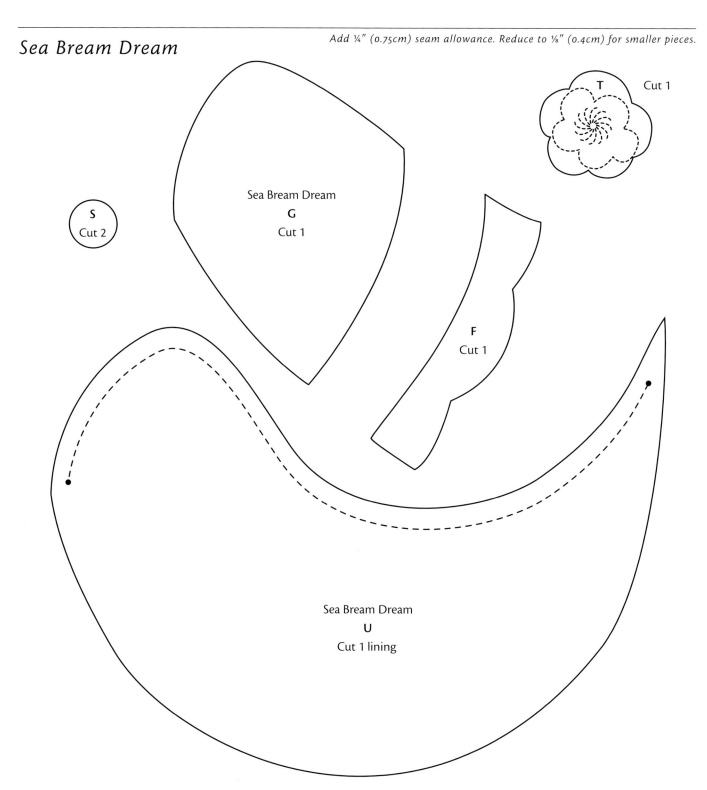

T
Cut 1

S
Cut 2

Sea Bream Dream
G
Cut 1

F
Cut 1

Sea Bream Dream
U
Cut 1 lining

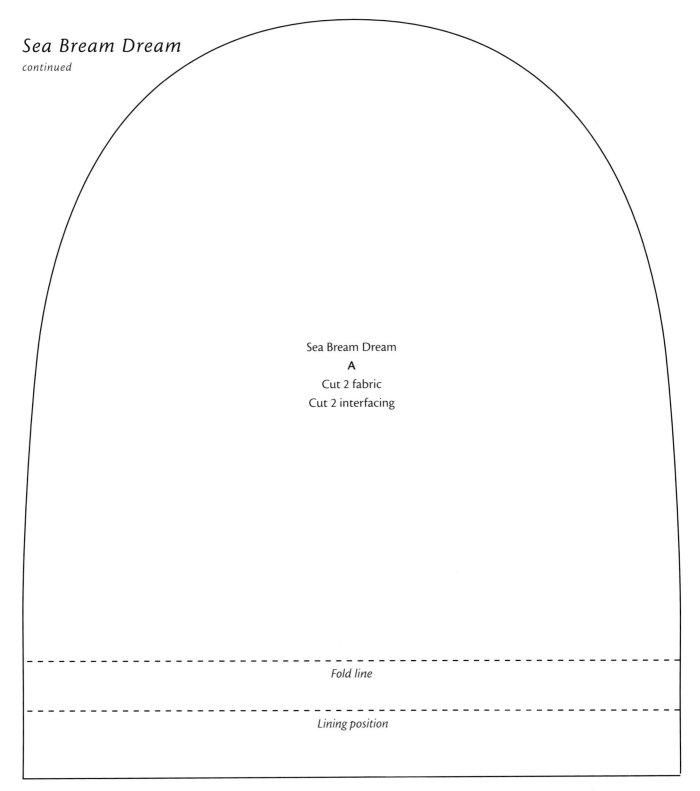

Sea Bream Dream
continued

Sea Bream Dream
A
Cut 2 fabric
Cut 2 interfacing

Fold line

Lining position

Sea Bream Dream

continued

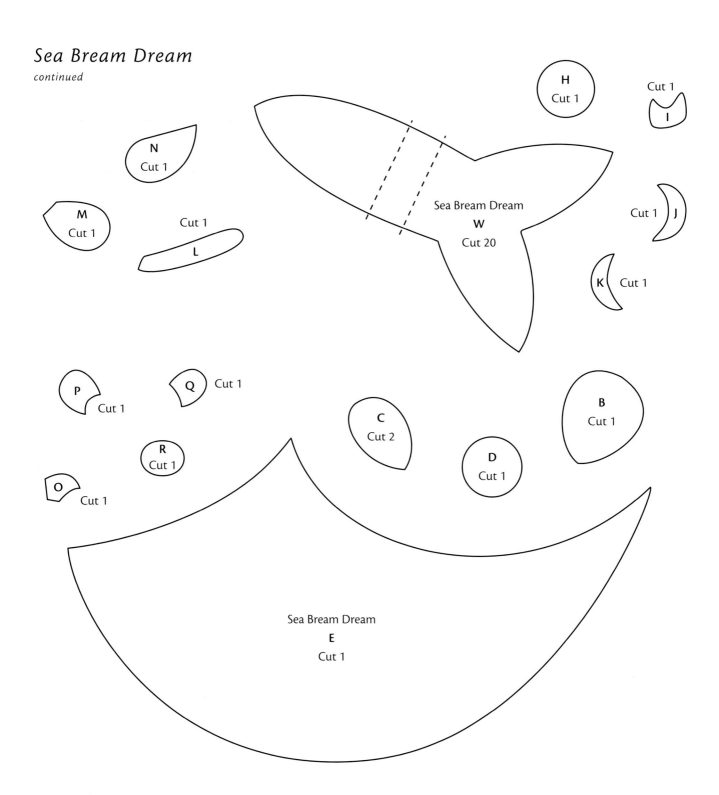

H
Cut 1

Cut 1
I

N
Cut 1

Sea Bream Dream
W
Cut 20

Cut 1   J

M
Cut 1

Cut 1
L

K   Cut 1

P
Cut 1

Q   Cut 1

C
Cut 2

B
Cut 1

R
Cut 1

D
Cut 1

O
Cut 1

Sea Bream Dream
E
Cut 1

Sea Bream Dream

continued

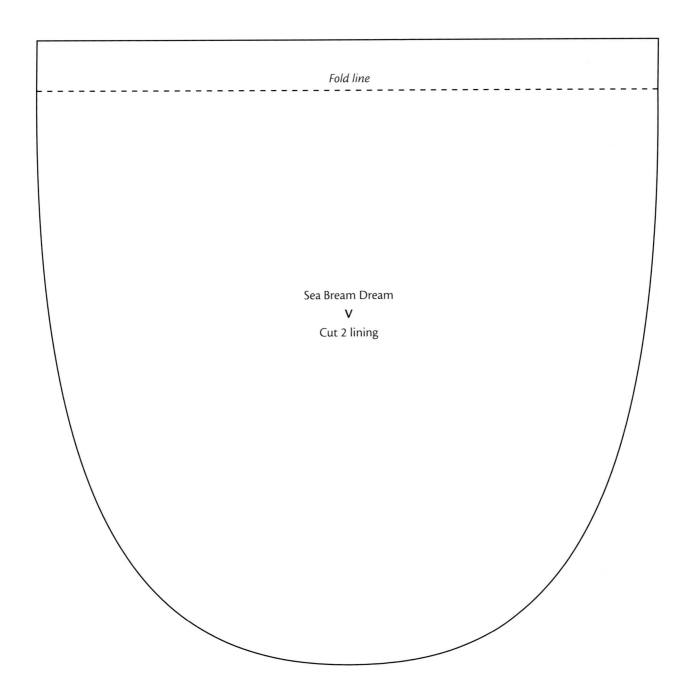

Fold line

Sea Bream Dream

∨

Cut 2 lining

Temari

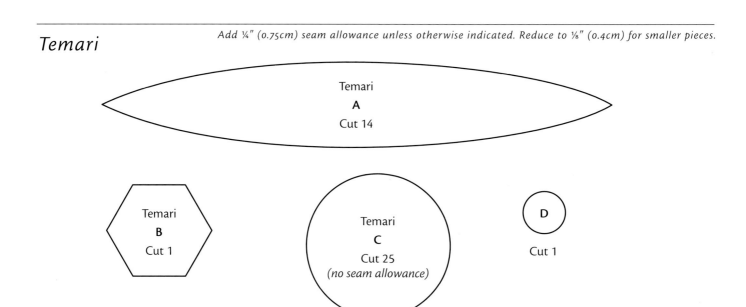

Temari
A
Cut 14

Temari
B
Cut 1

Temari
C
Cut 25
(no seam allowance)

D
Cut 1

Dutch Cat

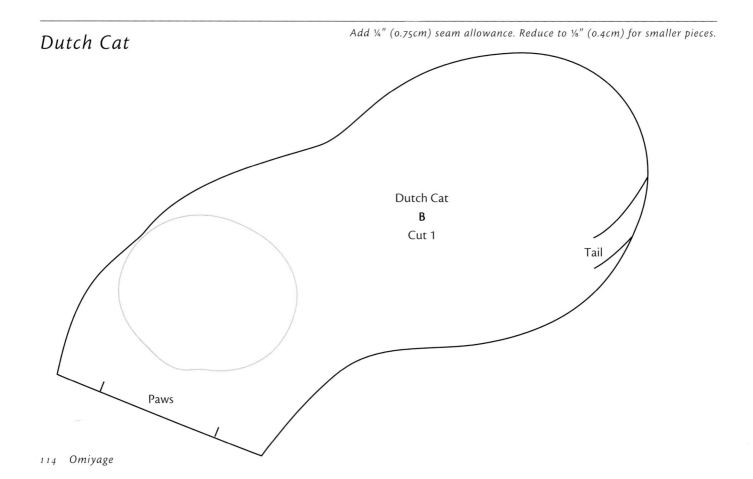

Dutch Cat
B
Cut 1

Tail

Paws

Dutch Cat
continued

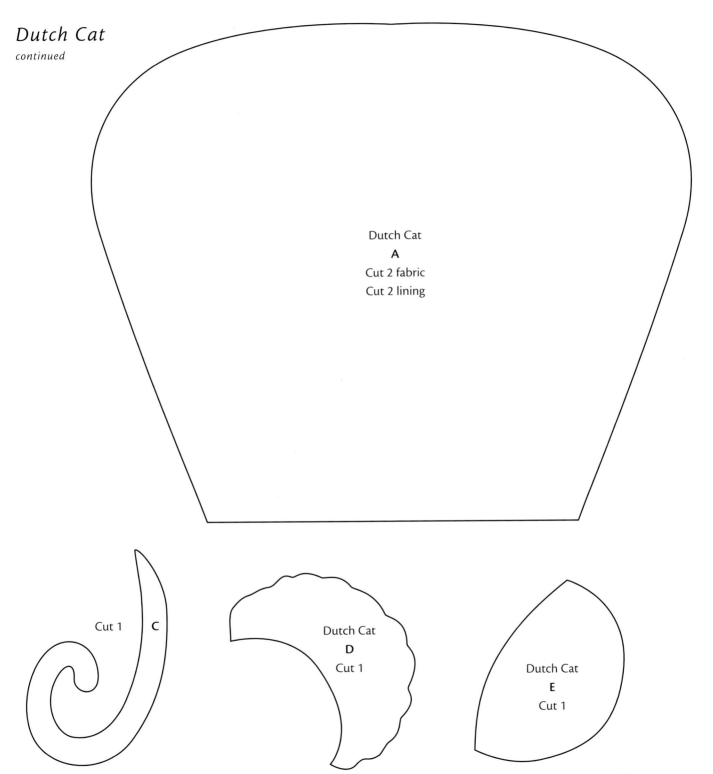

Dutch Cat
A
Cut 2 fabric
Cut 2 lining

Cut 1 **C**

Dutch Cat
D
Cut 1

Dutch Cat
E
Cut 1

Dutch Cat

continued

H
Cut 2

I
Cut 2

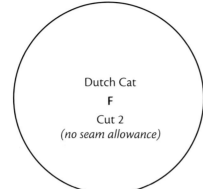

Dutch Cat
F
Cut 2
(no seam allowance)

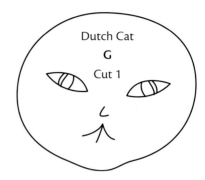

Dutch Cat
G
Cut 1

Oyster

Add ¼" (0.75cm) seam allowance unless otherwise indicated.

Oyster
B
Cut 1
(no seam allowance)

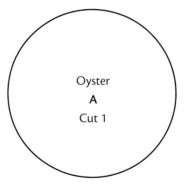

Oyster
A
Cut 1

Empress

Add ¼" (0.75cm) seam allowance. Reduce to ⅛" (0.4cm) for smaller pieces.

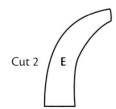

Cut 2 **E**

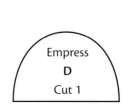

Empress
C
Cut 2

Empress
D
Cut 1

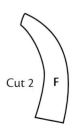

Cut 2 **F**

Empress

continued

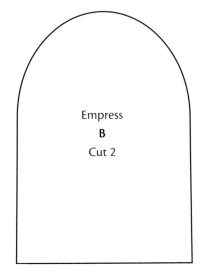

Empress
B
Cut 2

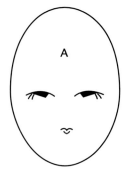

A

Cut 1 cardboard
(no seam allowance)
Cut 1 white cotton

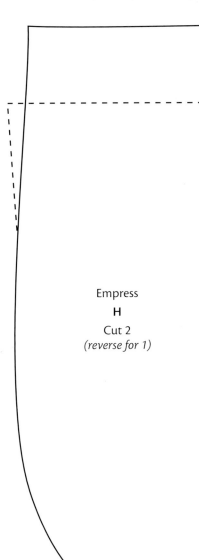

Empress
H
Cut 2
(reverse for 1)

Empress
G
Cut 1

Empress
continued

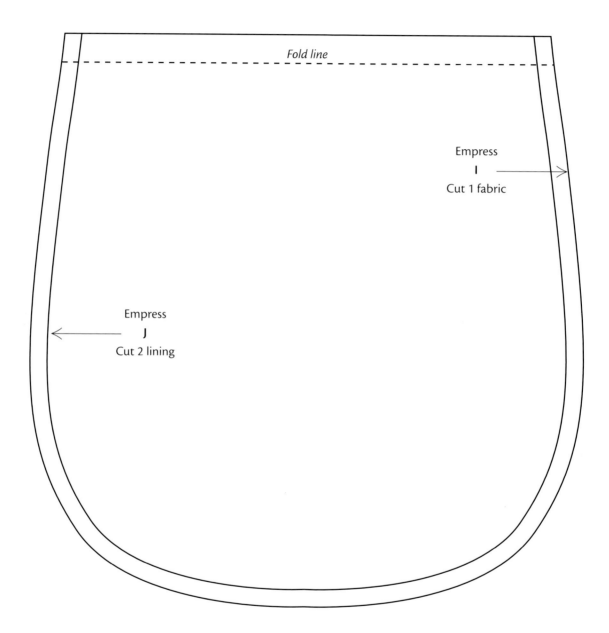

Fold line

Empress
I
Cut 1 fabric

Empress
J
Cut 2 lining

Conpaito

Add ¼" (0.75cm) seam allowance.

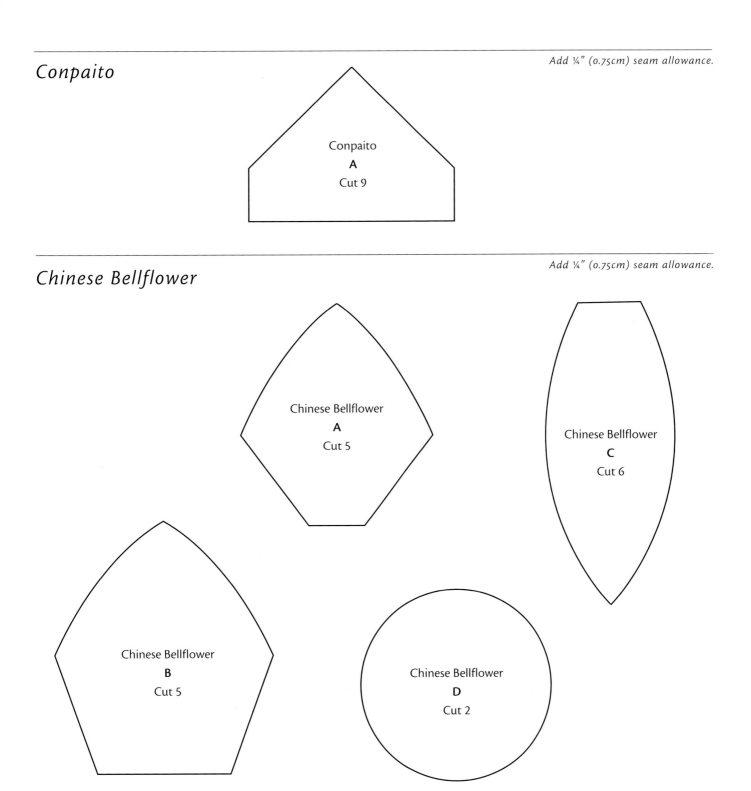

Conpaito
A
Cut 9

Chinese Bellflower

Add ¼" (0.75cm) seam allowance.

Chinese Bellflower
A
Cut 5

Chinese Bellflower
C
Cut 6

Chinese Bellflower
B
Cut 5

Chinese Bellflower
D
Cut 2

Camellia

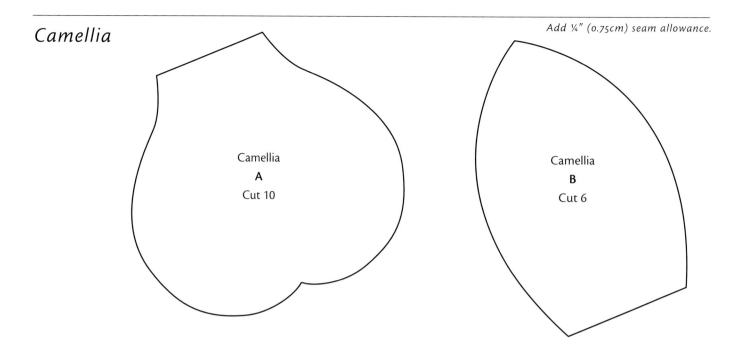

Camellia
A
Cut 10

Camellia
B
Cut 6

Cosmos

Add ¼" (0.75cm) seam allowance. Reduce to ⅛" (0.4cm) for smaller pieces.

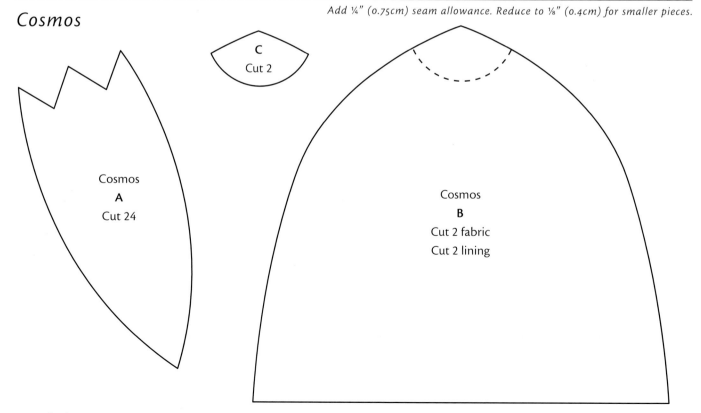

C
Cut 2

Cosmos
A
Cut 24

Cosmos
B
Cut 2 fabric
Cut 2 lining

Daffodil

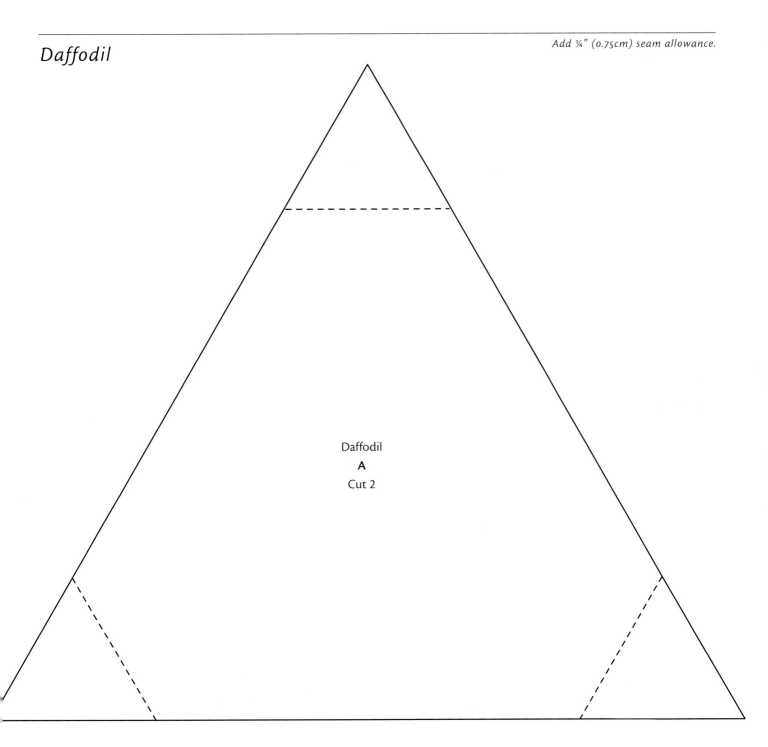

Daffodil

A

Cut 2

Add ¼" (0.75cm) seam allowance.

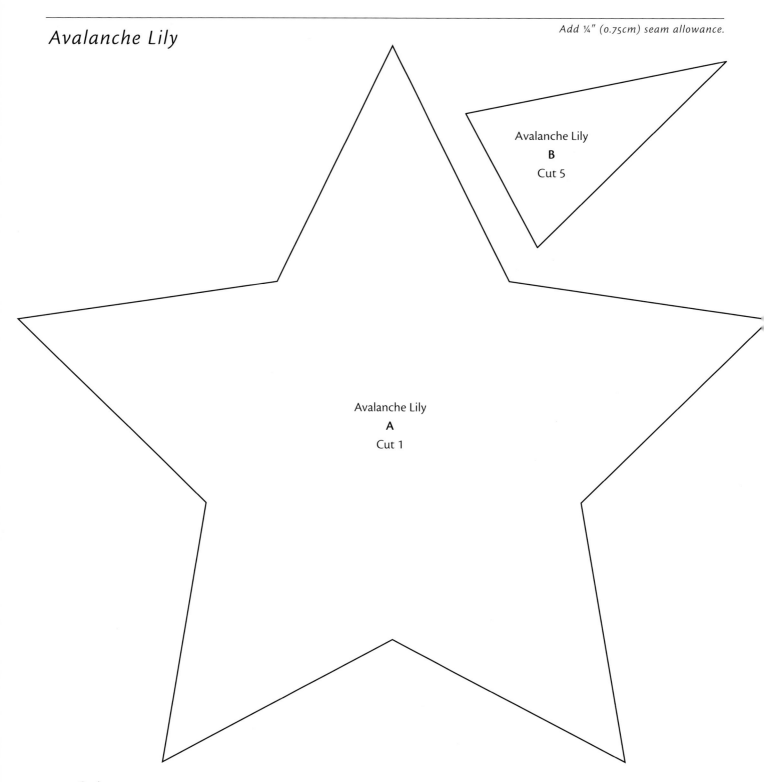

Avalanche Lily
B
Cut 5

Avalanche Lily
A
Cut 1

Sakura

Add ¼" (0.75cm) seam allowance.

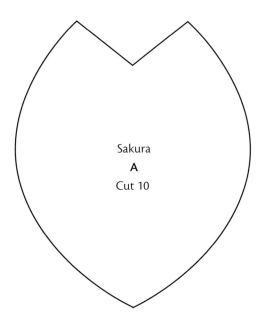

Sakura
A
Cut 10

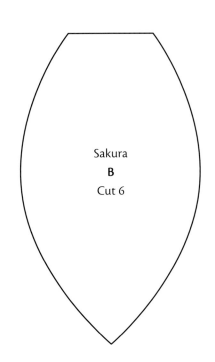

Sakura
B
Cut 6

Double Petal Sakura

Add ¼" (0.75cm) seam allowance.

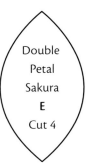

Double
Petal
Sakura
E
Cut 4

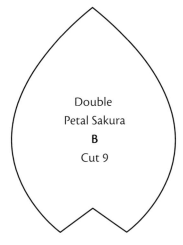

Double
Petal Sakura
B
Cut 9

Double Petal Sakura
continued

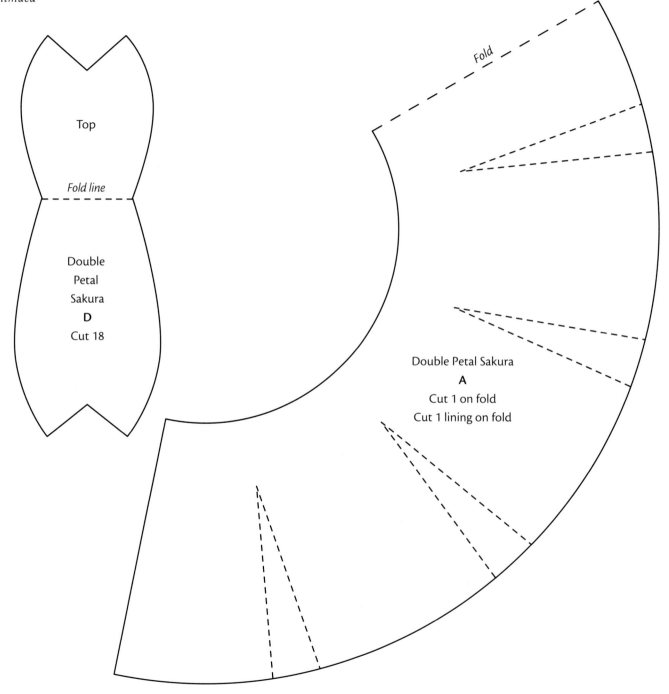

Top

Fold line

Double
Petal
Sakura
D
Cut 18

Fold

Double Petal Sakura
A
Cut 1 on fold
Cut 1 lining on fold

Double Petal Sakura

continued

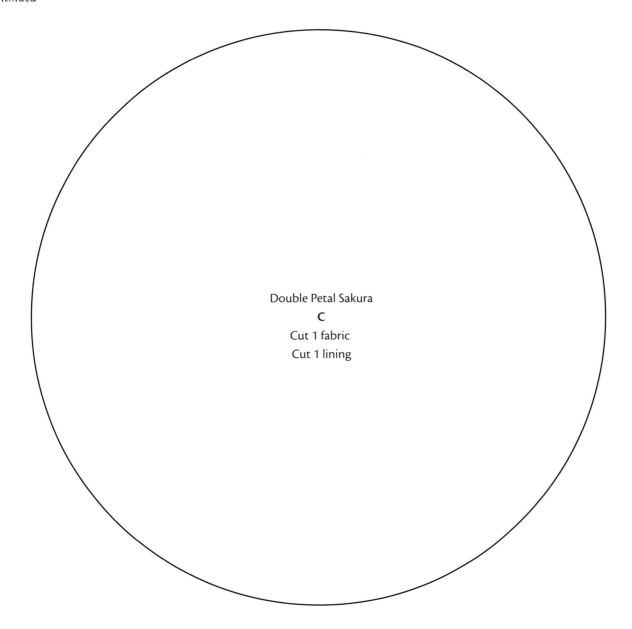

Double Petal Sakura
C
Cut 1 fabric
Cut 1 lining

Raindrop

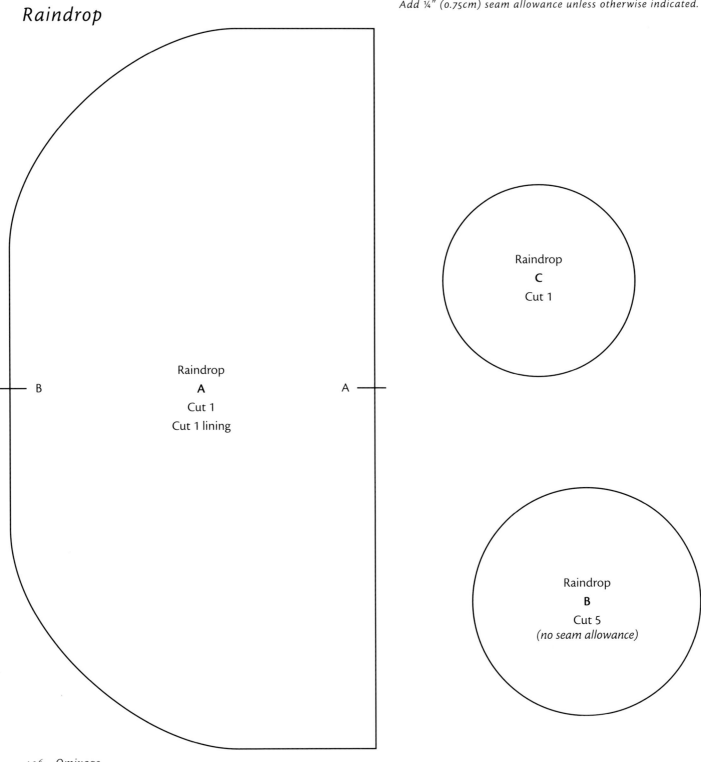

Raindrop
A
Cut 1
Cut 1 lining

B

A

Raindrop
C
Cut 1

Raindrop
B
Cut 5
(no seam allowance)

Village Girl

Add ¼" (0.75cm) seam allowance.

Village Girl

D

Cut 1

A

Cut 2

Village Girl
continued

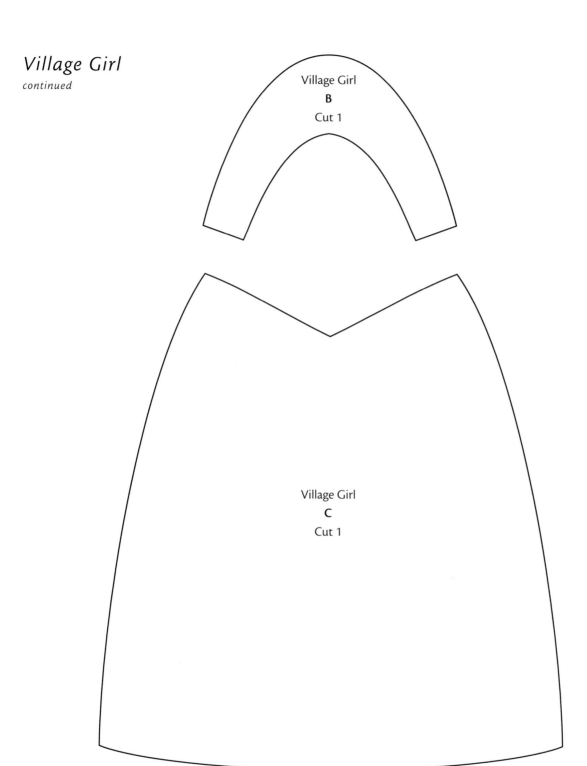

Village Girl
B
Cut 1

Village Girl
C
Cut 1

Village Girl
continued

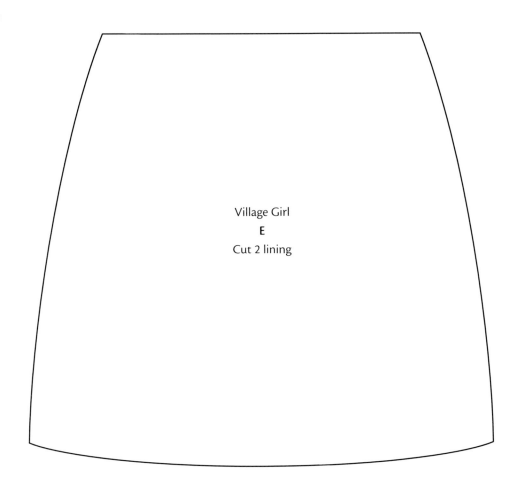

Village Girl
E
Cut 2 lining

Pretty Princess

Add ¼" (0.75cm) seam allowance.

Pretty Princess
A
Cut 1

Playtime!

Playtime!
C
Cut 1

Playtime!
A
Cut 1
(no seam allowance)

Playtime!
B
Cut 1 cardboard
(no seam allowance)
Cut 1 fabric

Playtime!
(variation)
D
Cut 1

Boy Acrobat

Add ¼" (0.75cm) seam allowance. Reduce to ⅛" (0.4cm) for smaller pieces.

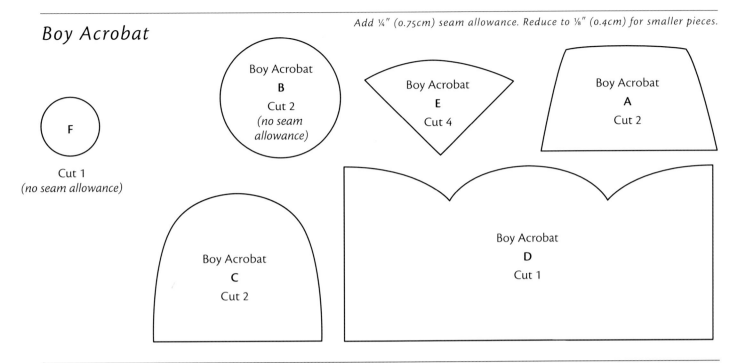

F

Cut 1
(no seam allowance)

Boy Acrobat
B
Cut 2
(no seam allowance)

Boy Acrobat
E
Cut 4

Boy Acrobat
A
Cut 2

Boy Acrobat
C
Cut 2

Boy Acrobat
D
Cut 1

Pocket Baby

Add ¼" (0.75cm) seam allowance.

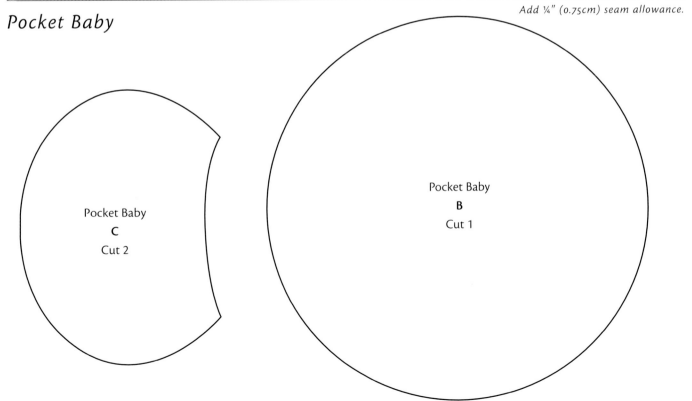

Pocket Baby
C
Cut 2

Pocket Baby
B
Cut 1

Pocket Baby

continued

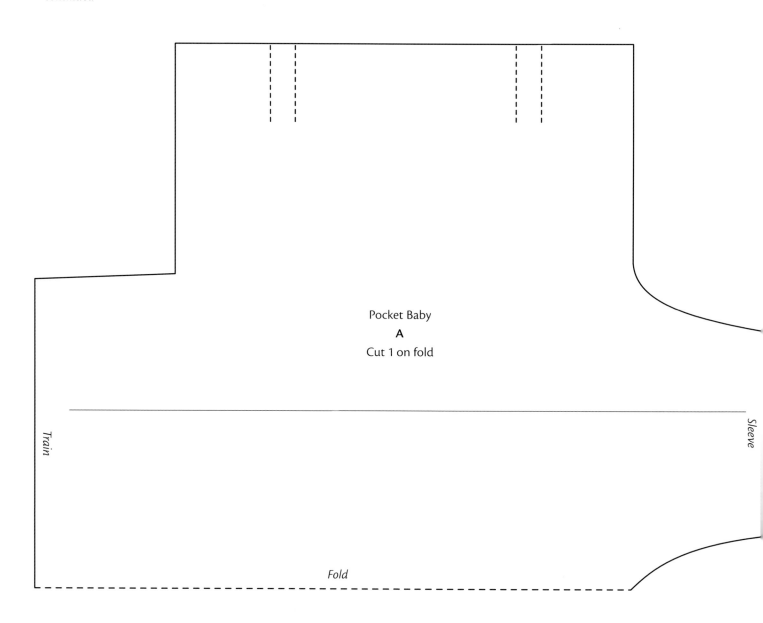

Pocket Baby

A

Cut 1 on fold

Train

Sleeve

Fold

Little Teapot

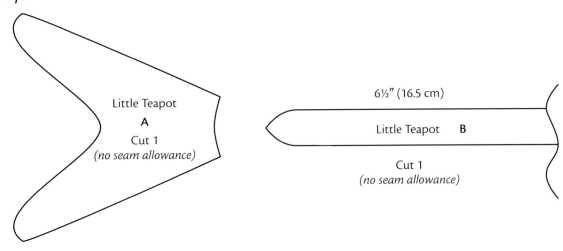

Little Teapot
A
Cut 1
(no seam allowance)

6½" (16.5 cm)

Little Teapot   **B**

Cut 1
(no seam allowance)

Sewing Box

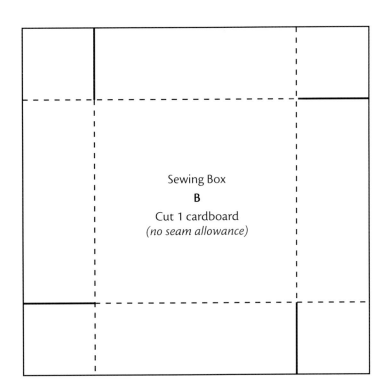

Sewing Box
B
Cut 1 cardboard
(no seam allowance)

Sewing Box

continued

Sewing Box

A

Cut 1 cardboard
(no seam allowance)

Cut 1 fabric
(⅜" [1 cm] seam allowance)

Cherry Surprise

Add ¼" (0.75cm) seam allowance unless otherwise indicated.

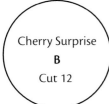

Cherry Surprise
B
Cut 12

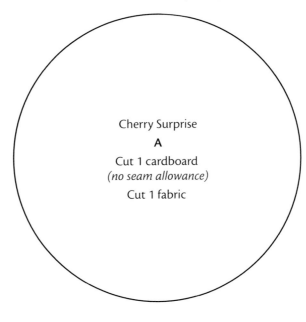

Cherry Surprise
A
Cut 1 cardboard
(no seam allowance)
Cut 1 fabric

D

Cut 12
(no seam allowance)

Flower Box

Add ¼" (0.75cm) seam allowance unless otherwise indicated.

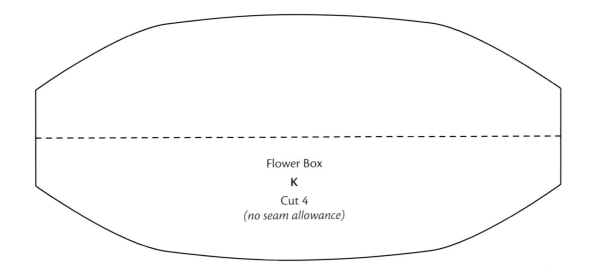

Flower Box
K
Cut 4
(no seam allowance)

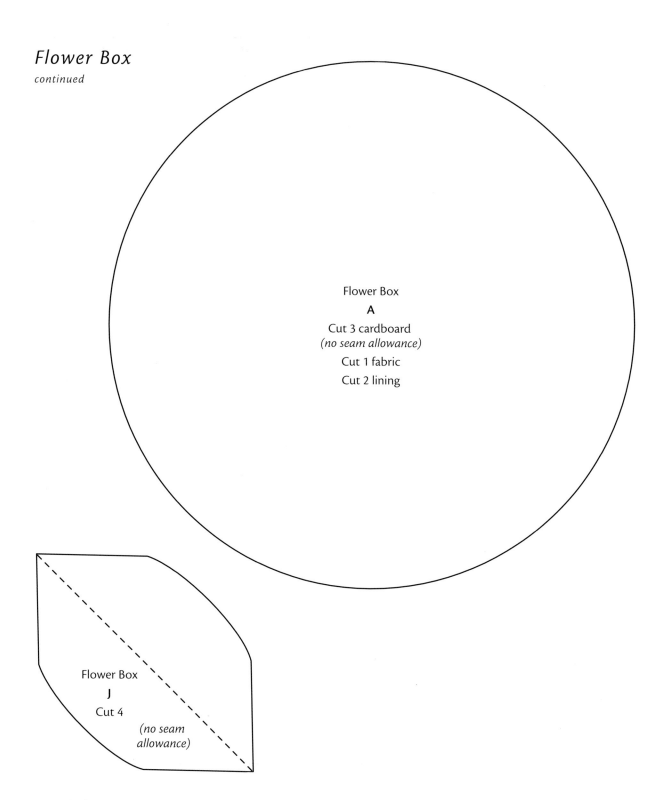

Flower Box

A

Cut 3 cardboard
(no seam allowance)

Cut 1 fabric

Cut 2 lining

Flower Box

J

Cut 4

*(no seam
allowance)*

Eleganz

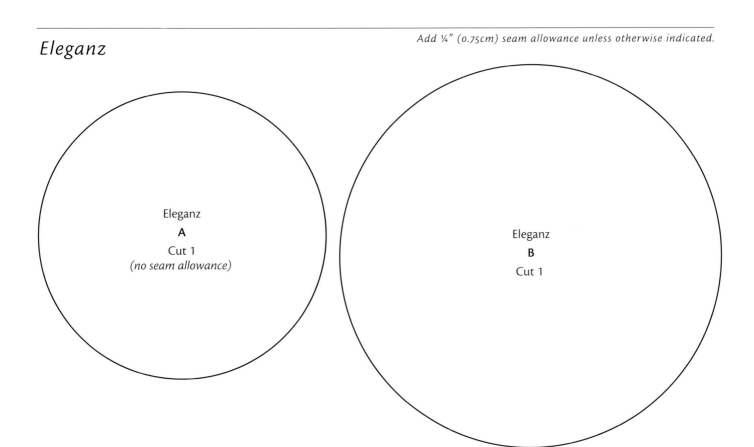

Eleganz
A
Cut 1
(no seam allowance)

Eleganz
B
Cut 1

Ko Bukuro

Add ¼" (0.75cm) seam allowance.

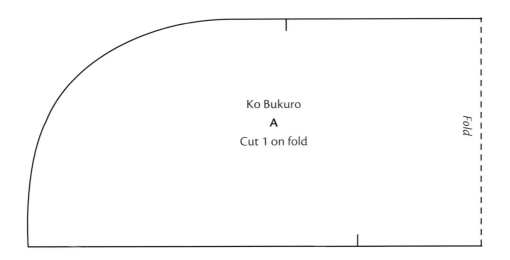

Ko Bukuro
A
Cut 1 on fold

Fold

Edo Temari

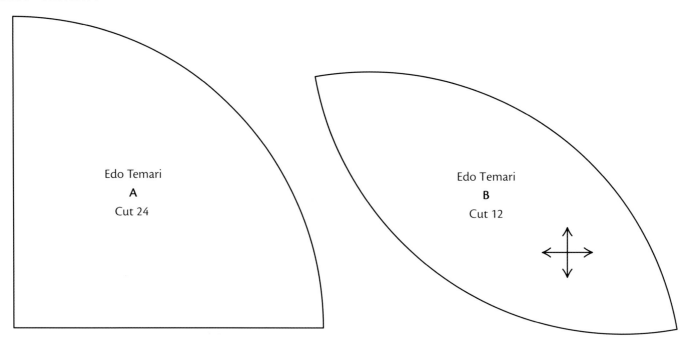

Edo Temari
A
Cut 24

Edo Temari
B
Cut 12

Kusadama

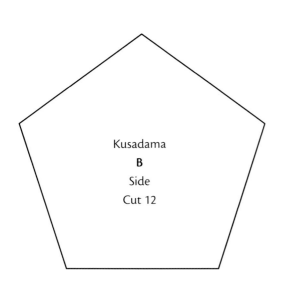

Kusadama
B
Side
Cut 12

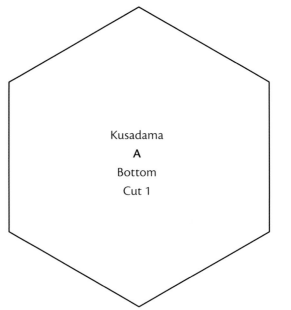

Kusadama
A
Bottom
Cut 1

Pandora

Add ¼" (0.75cm) seam allowance unless otherwise indicated.

Pandora
A
Cut 4 cardboard
(no seam allowance)
Cut 2 fabric
Cut 2 lining

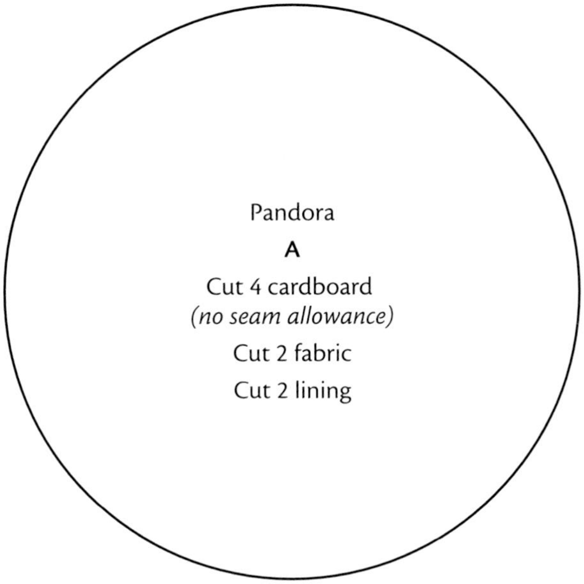

Fortune Catcher

Add ¼" (0.75cm) seam allowance unless otherwise indicated.

Fortune Catcher
A
Cut 2 cardboard
(no seam allowance)
Cut 1 fabric

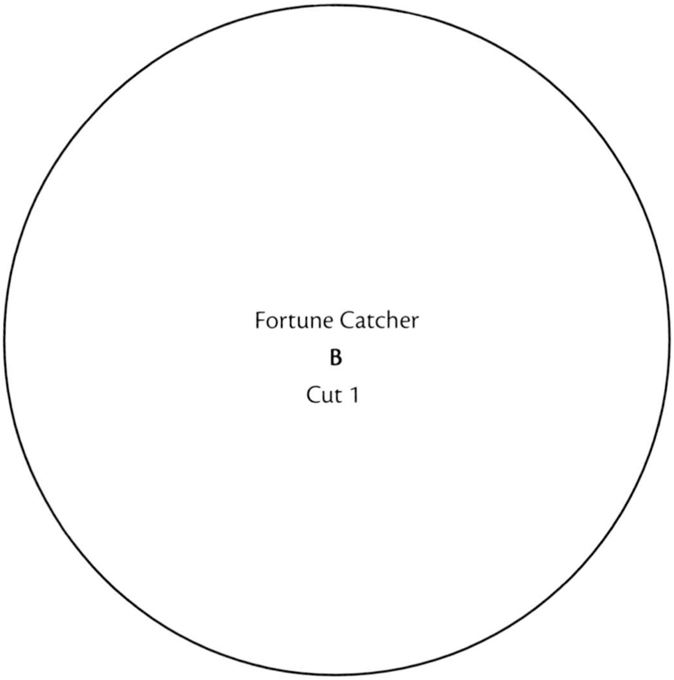

Fortune Catcher
B
Cut 1

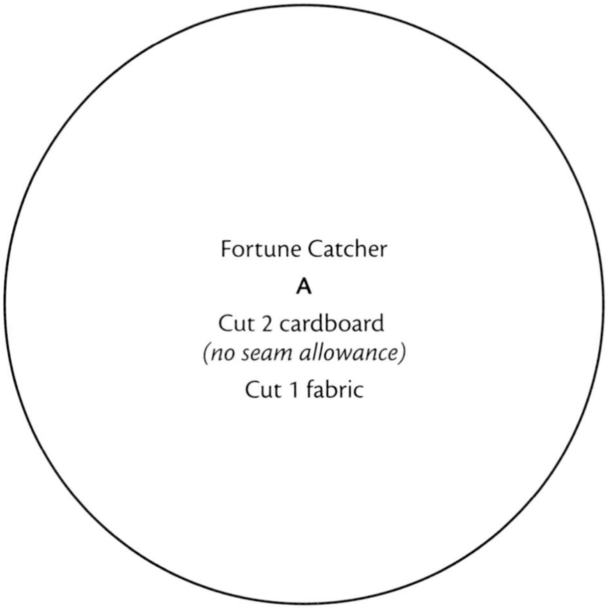

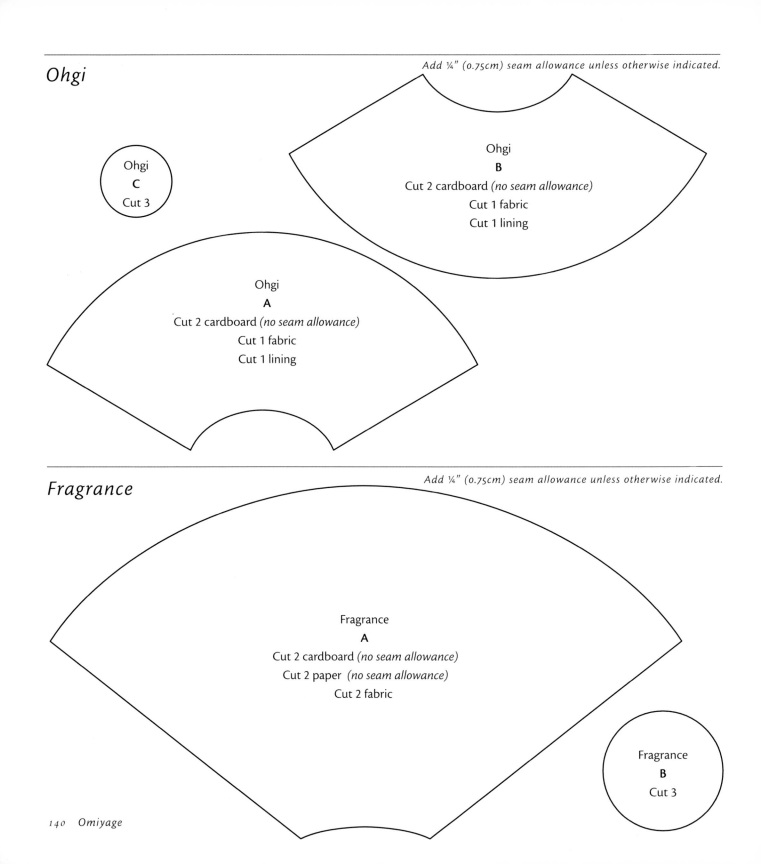

Ohgi

Ohgi
C
Cut 3

Ohgi
B
Cut 2 cardboard (*no seam allowance*)
Cut 1 fabric
Cut 1 lining

Ohgi
A
Cut 2 cardboard (*no seam allowance*)
Cut 1 fabric
Cut 1 lining

Fragrance

Fragrance
A
Cut 2 cardboard (*no seam allowance*)
Cut 2 paper (*no seam allowance*)
Cut 2 fabric

Fragrance
B
Cut 3

Butterfly

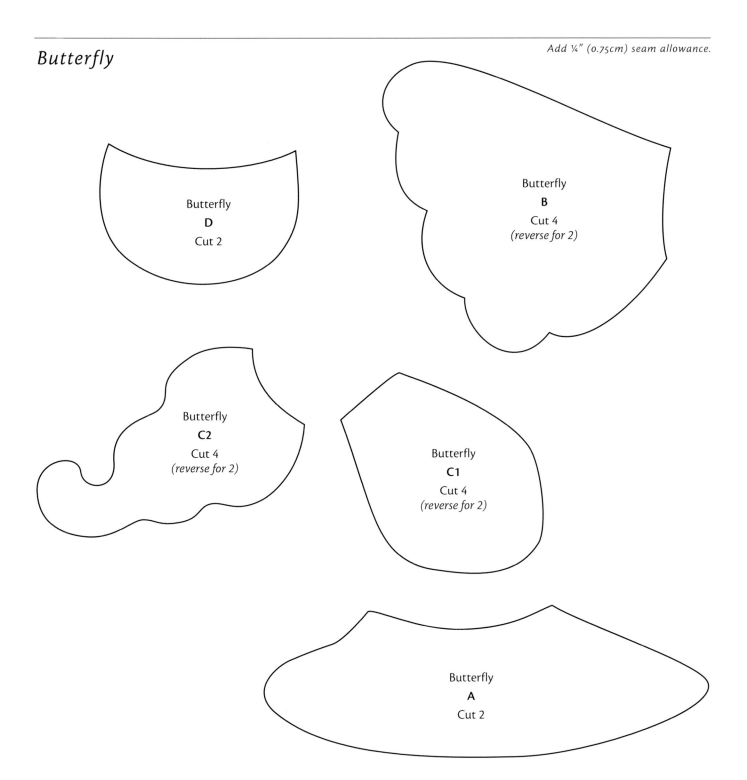

Butterfly
D
Cut 2

Butterfly
B
Cut 4
(reverse for 2)

Butterfly
C2
Cut 4
(reverse for 2)

Butterfly
C1
Cut 4
(reverse for 2)

Butterfly
A
Cut 2

Pine Cone

Add ¼" (0.75cm) seam allowance.

Pine cone
A
Cut 7

Sparrow

Add ¼" (0.75cm) seam allowance.

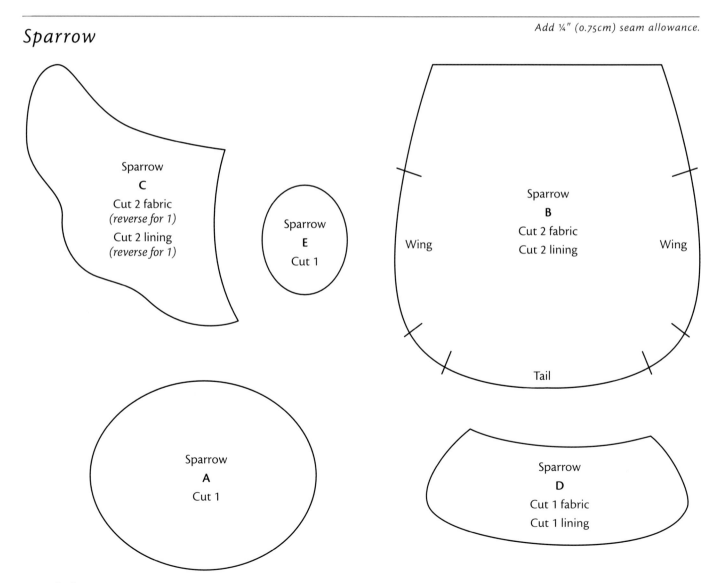

Sparrow
C
Cut 2 fabric
(reverse for 1)
Cut 2 lining
(reverse for 1)

Sparrow
E
Cut 1

Sparrow
B
Cut 2 fabric
Cut 2 lining

Wing

Wing

Tail

Sparrow
A
Cut 1

Sparrow
D
Cut 1 fabric
Cut 1 lining

Squirrel

Add ¼" (0.75cm) seam allowance unless otherwise indicated. Reduce to ⅛" (0.4cm) for smaller pieces.

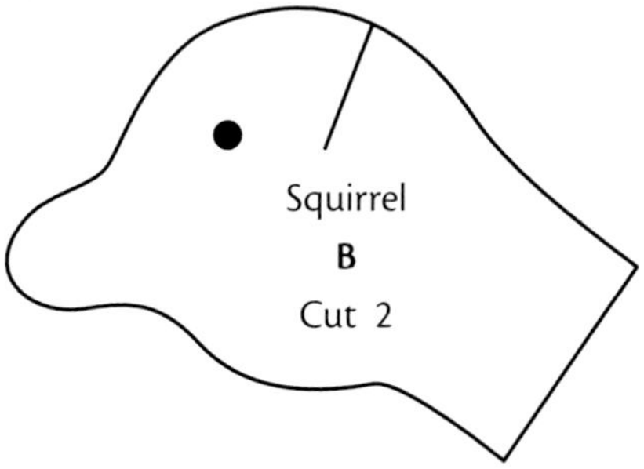

Squirrel
B
Cut 2

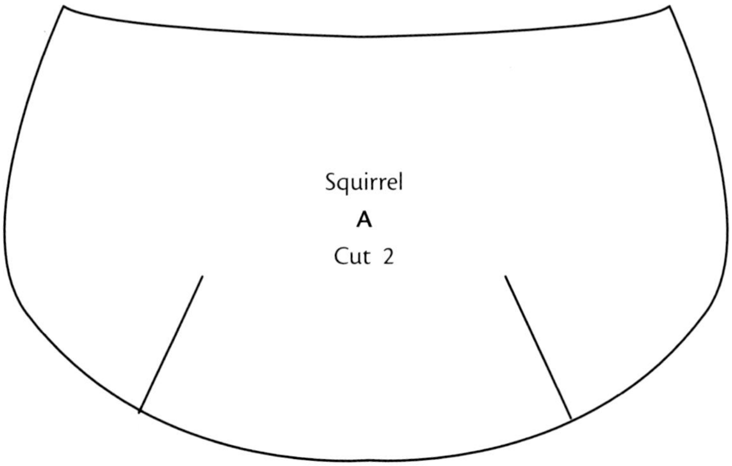

Squirrel
A
Cut 2

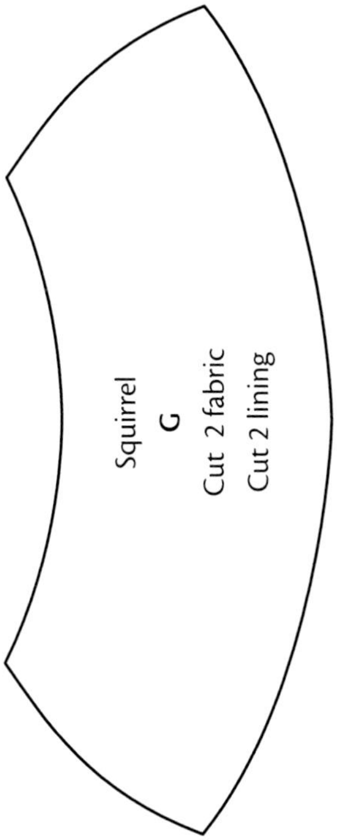

Squirrel
F
Cut 2 lining

Squirrel
G
Cut 2 fabric
Cut 2 lining

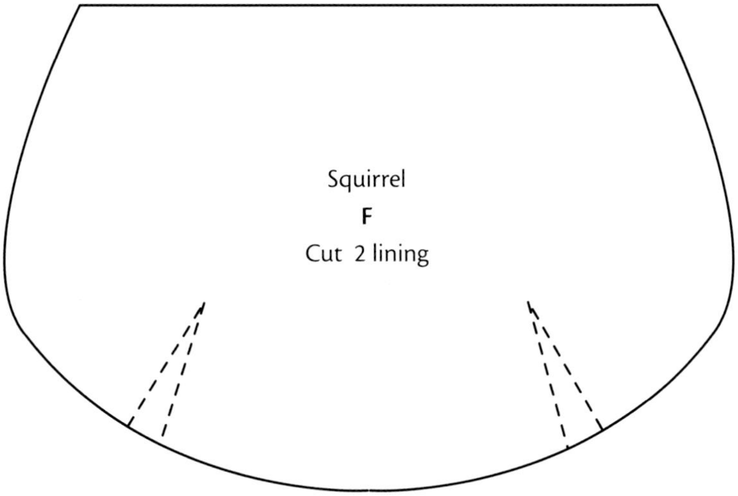

Squirrel

continued

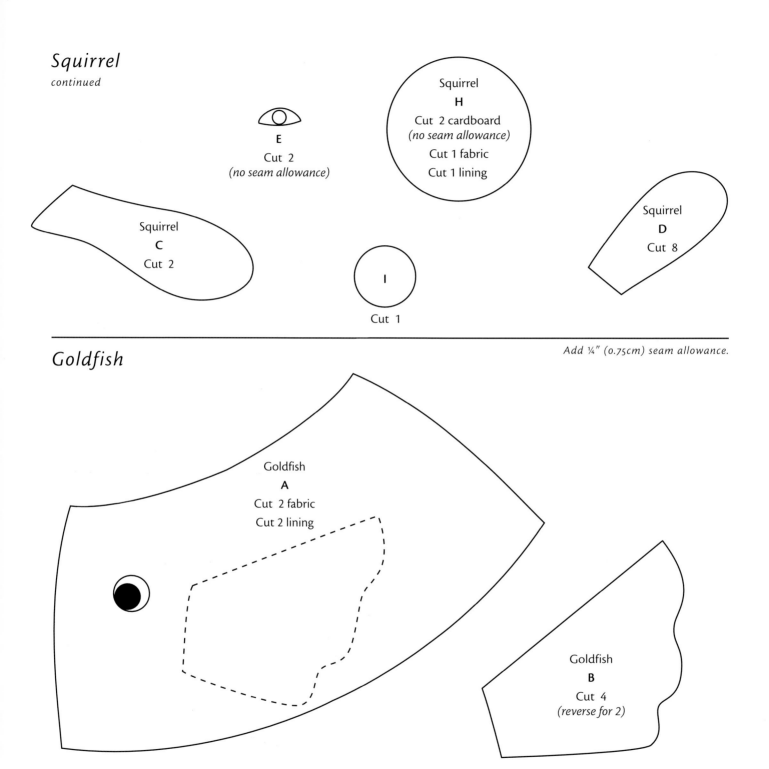

E

Cut 2
(no seam allowance)

Squirrel
H

Cut 2 cardboard
(no seam allowance)

Cut 1 fabric

Cut 1 lining

Squirrel
C

Cut 2

Squirrel
D

Cut 8

I

Cut 1

Goldfish

Add ¼" (0.75cm) seam allowance.

Goldfish
A

Cut 2 fabric

Cut 2 lining

Goldfish
B

Cut 4
(reverse for 2)

Goldfish
continued

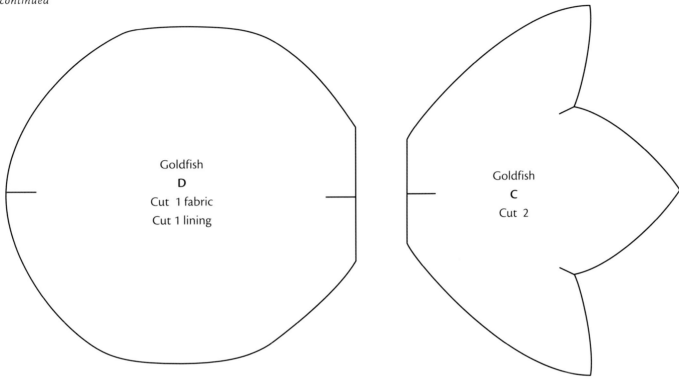

Goldfish
D
Cut 1 fabric
Cut 1 lining

Goldfish
C
Cut 2

Add ¼" (0.75cm) seam allowance unless otherwise indicated.

Cicada

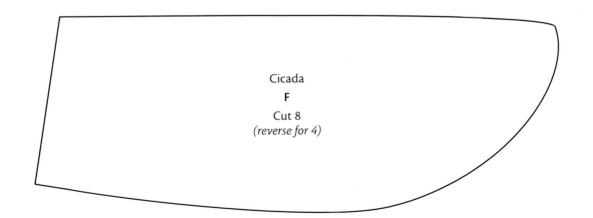

Cicada
F
Cut 8
(reverse for 4)

Cicada

continued

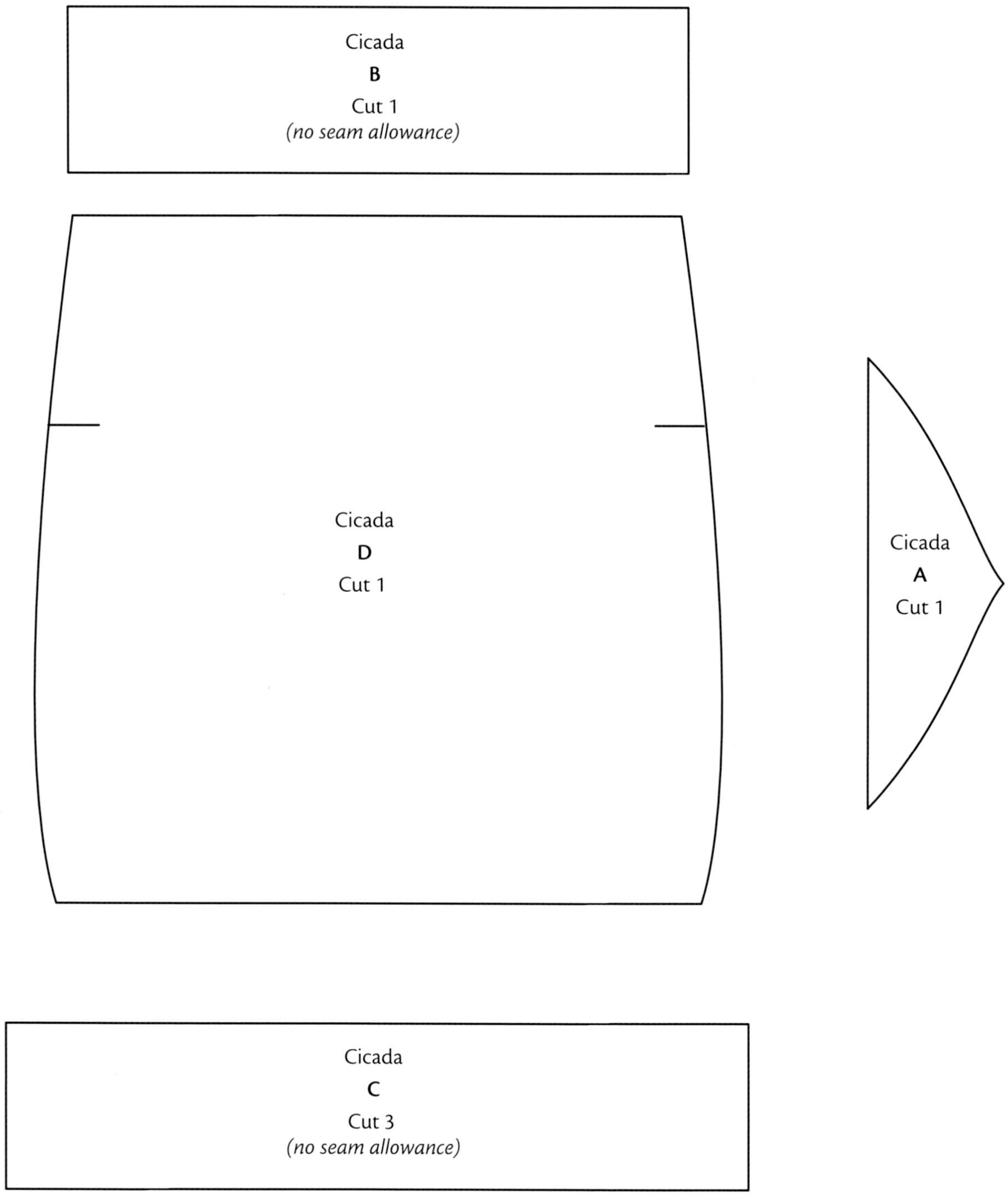

Cicada

B

Cut 1

(no seam allowance)

Cicada

D

Cut 1

Cicada

A

Cut 1

Cicada

C

Cut 3

(no seam allowance)

Cicada

continued

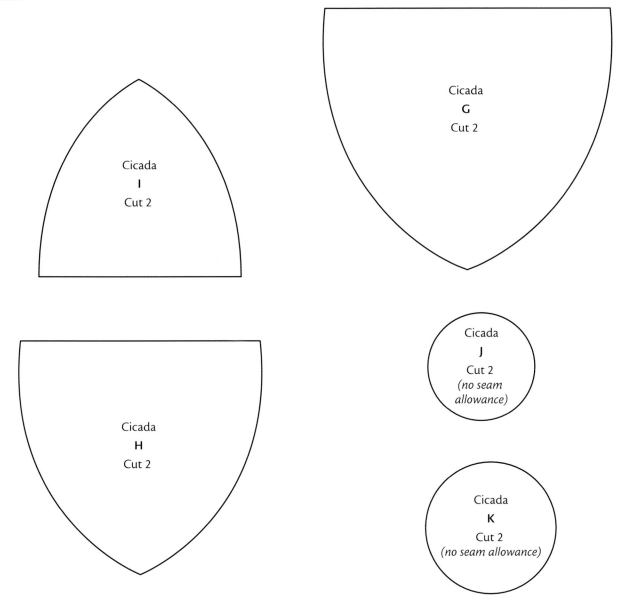

Cicada
I
Cut 2

Cicada
G
Cut 2

Cicada
H
Cut 2

Cicada
J
Cut 2
(no seam allowance)

Cicada
K
Cut 2
(no seam allowance)

Cicada
continued

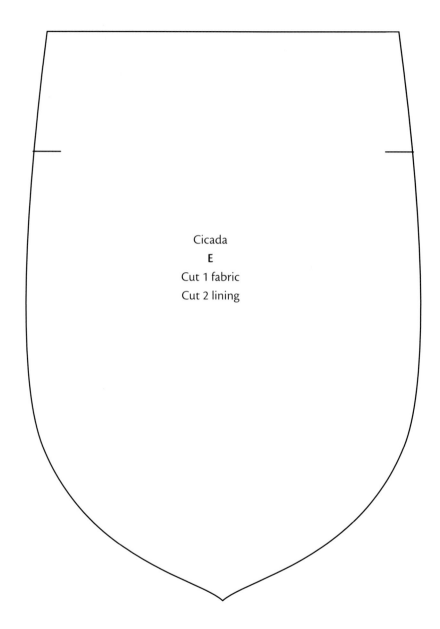

Cicada
E
Cut 1 fabric
Cut 2 lining

Bunny

Add ¼" (0.75cm) seam allowance unless otherwise indicated.

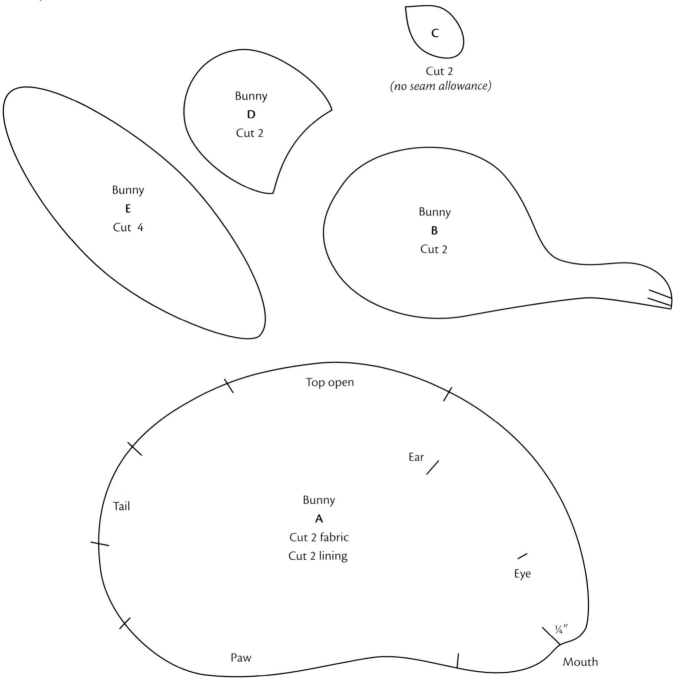

C
Cut 2
(no seam allowance)

Bunny
D
Cut 2

Bunny
E
Cut 4

Bunny
B
Cut 2

Top open

Ear

Tail

Bunny
A
Cut 2 fabric
Cut 2 lining

Eye

¼"

Paw

Mouth

Teaching Omiyage

Lesson Plan:
Chinese Bellflower

Chinese Bellflower *is pictured on the cover of* Omiyage. *A version in an entirely different set of fabrics is shown here and on page 26. During this sample lesson, students will make this elegant flower pouch. The lesson is ideal for a half-day workshop.*

Most of the flowers featured in Chapter 2 are constructed in a similar way. If you prefer, however, you can choose the easiest of the flower designs, *Daffodil* on page 31, or one that is a little more challenging, such as *Camellia* on pages 29 and 30 or *Sakura* on pages 35 and 36.

The process of making any of the flower pouches in Chapter 2 includes tracing and cutting from templates and practicing a precise method of stitching that can be done either by hand or by machine. Several also include a form of fabric origami. This workshop also encourages students to look at colors and fabrics in a new way.

Whichever flower you choose, make up at least three versions before class begins. The more samples you make, the easier it will be for students to envisage how their flowers will look in colors and fabrics of their choosing. Consider making up project kits for each student in a choice of fabrics that reflect the fabrics in your samples (see next page).

The lesson plan works well for a half-day workshop. You can also use it for two shorter two-hour classes. If you are worried about running out of time, have students choose fabrics before class. If they have sewn before, have them cut out the pattern pieces ahead of time.

Introduction

Show students your samples and the photographs of *Chinese Bellflower* in *Omiyage*. Show the hidden pouch underneath the flower. Discuss color and fabric selection, showing that the project uses up to eight different fabrics (flower center, flower petals, underside of petals, leaves, underside of leaves, lining, hem, beads). Talk about color combinations, color contrast, texture, and the scale of patterned fabrics. Let students choose from the kits you have prepared or let them select from a limited number of bolts in a variety of colors and prints. If students have brought their own fabric scraps, help them choose complementary fabrics that will work well with their choices. Read through all directions for *Chinese Bellflower* on pages 25 and 26.

Cutting Pattern Pieces

Hand out photocopies of the pattern pieces on page 119 or have students trace the patterns. Point out that the patterns do not include seam allowances. Have students use sharp scissors to cut out each piece and pin them onto selected fabrics, right side up. Have students draw carefully around each piece with a quilter's pencil, lightly marking the seam lines. Have them cut around each piece, ¼" (0.75cm) away from the seam lines. Note that Pattern D does not require seam allowance—students simply cut on the marked lines. Note also that students will need to cut the petals and leaves one at a time and then reuse the pattern. Students will need to cut a total of:

Pattern A (petals)	Cut 5
Pattern B (underside of petals)	Cut 5
Pattern C (top and bottom leaves)	Cut 3 in each of two fabrics for total of 6 pieces
Pattern D (fabric beads)	Cut 2 (do not add seam allowance)

In addition, students will need measure and cut strips of fabric in the following dimensions. Explain that these measurements already include seam allowances:

Center flower	Cut 1	1" × 3¼" (2.8cm × 8.5cm)
Pocket lining	Cut 2	2½" × 7½" (6.5cm × 19.4cm)
Hem	Cut 2	1½" × 4½" (4cm × 11.6cm)

Sewing

Explain that the project can be made either by hand or by machine. However, since the pattern pieces are small, machine stitching does not save a lot of time. Students may find it easier to manipulate smaller pieces of fabric and to stitch curves by hand.

Follow Steps 1 to 5 to create flower design. Demonstrate a simple running stitch in Step 1 and a gather-stitch in Step 2. Stress the importance of stitching precisely on the sewing lines students marked on their pattern pieces, leaving an even ¼″ (0.75cm) seam allowance all around.

Follow Steps 6 and 7 to create the inner pouch and Step 8 to make the leaves. Review the directions on page xvi for making the hem, pointing out that all the flower designs and several other projects in *Omiyage* use exactly the same technique.

Finishing

Explain that on pages xvii to xviii there are five different methods for making fabric beads, and each has a slightly different appearance. If they do not wish to make the fabric beads in Step 10, students can use purchased beads instead. Have them choose ribbons and beads to finish off their designs.

Planning an Extended Classroom Schedule

You can use *Omiyage* as the basis for a series of six or more two-hour classes. To make the best use of class time, ask students to cut out their pattern pieces ahead of time. However, if you do this, you may wish to devote a shorter introductory class to choosing fabrics and preparing and cutting patterns.

The class sequence suggested here is designed to allow students to start off with very simple projects and practice their skills as they move on to make more challenging ones.

Class 1

Skills: Straight seams, cutting templates, stitching curves

Select from: *Daffodil*, page 31

Tsuru, page 99

Panache!, pages 4 and 5

Class 2

Skills: Making pouches, hem stitch

Select from: *Cosmos*, page 33

Chrysanthemum, page 27

Pretty Princess, page 51

Class 3

Skills: Rotary cutting, piecing

Select from: *Marbles*, pages 2 and 3

Kusadama, pages 80 and 81

Class 4

Skills: Combining fabric with other materials

Select from: *Sewing Box*, pages 63 and 64

Temari, pages 12 and 13

Fortune Catcher, page 85

Class 5

Skills: Three-dimensional effects, Y-seam construction

Select from: *Conpaito*, pages 20 and 21

Candy Twist, pages 10 and 11

Pine Cone, pages 94 and 95

Class 6

Skills: Knots, embellishments

Select from: *Playtime!*, pages 52 to 55

Pandora, pages 83 and 84

Sea Bream Dream, pages 7 to 9